PTSD

Plus

Understanding and Treating the Trauma of Military Service and Beyond

BY

CARL W. MOHLER

Printed in the United States of America

Published By Blackmount Publishing

Table of Contents

Introduction

Americans have struggled with the concept of PTSD for almost four decades at this point (Tull, 2020). Commonly known as "shell shock", the full impact of PTSD has become clearer and more transparent throughout the generations. At various points, tests for PTSD have been rendered, and what has been made clear is that PTSD will be a struggle for many Vietnam Veterans for many years to come. There are many issues that PTSD can affect, such as substance abuse, which can lead to self-medication. There can be a connection to pain. Many veterans have to face issues with chronic pain, which can worsen, leading to depression and increased pain.

There is also a connection between PTSD and depression. Over half of the people experiencing clinical depression also experience PTSD. PTSD is also a risk factor for heart disease. People with PTSD are also at risk for diabetes, which can also affect heart disease. The bottom line for PTSD is to recognize the negative impact it can have on a person's daily life. The war is not over for any person who has been diagnosed with PTSD, but the journey is moving forward. There is so much more to PTSD at this point.

Post-Traumatic Stress Disorder, or PTSD, is a mental health condition that is triggered by a terrifying event, either by experiencing or witnessing it. Symptoms may include flashbacks, nightmares, and severe anxiety, as well as uncontrollable thoughts about the event. What must be realized is that PTSD is a mental health issue that develops in some people who have experienced a shocking or scary event. It has been assumed that only veterans in wartime can get PTSD, but the truth of the matter is that almost anyone can get PTSD.

The Vietnam War

The Vietnam War was a struggle for control of Vietnam, a country in Southeast Asia. The Vietnam War displayed the limits of U.S. military power. Fifty-eight thousand Americans were killed, along with millions of civilians of South Vietnam. On one side was the Communist regime of North Vietnam, which sought to unite the two Vietnams under a Communist government. On the other side was the democratic government of South Vietnam with American military backing. What many people still struggle with forty years later is why so many young Americans died for a cause that we didn't openly support. The answer is not apparent, but it appears that America's 36th president, Lyndon B. Johnson, had some professional and personal issues that supported his belief that America should be involved in the Vietnam conflict.

The Vietnam Conflict was not officially a war for the U.S., in the sense that the President or Congress never requested a declaration of war. However, it was fought with the full strength of the American military. The conflict was fought by the full strength of the US Army, which included the National Guard. Combined with the other branches of the U.S. military, approximately 9 million young men and women were deployed over 10 years. The US Air Force deployed heavy bombers, attack aircraft, fighter bombers, and support forces. The US Navy deployed aircraft carriers, heavy cruisers, and even a battleship. The Marines, like the Army, operated from in-country bases. The Coast Guard patrolled the rivers and waterways.

Politicians of Peace

Lyndon Johnson came with impressive credentials. He was a Texan, a liberal Democrat, and a reformer who supported social and racial equality in America. However, he also pursued an aggressive foreign policy, including the rapid buildup of military forces in Vietnam. The Vietnam conflict was not only a learning experience for Johnson and the entire American political structure. America as a whole had to reexamine its commitment to fighting communism. The expense of losing a huge number of American lives was not justified. This whole issue, created by Vietnam, affected its own national identity. It cannot be doubted that the entire cultural and political structure was twisted around Vietnam. However, Johnson felt that America had an obligation to support South Vietnam.

It was thought that Johnson was a firm activist of the domino theory, which assumed that Communism would spread like wildfire if South Vietnam fell to the North. Johnson had issues with the entire affair, and he made some decisions. One of the most challenging actions was deploying military personnel to South Vietnam. This was clearly one of the least popular issues he had to address. Still, due to political convictions, this was something he pursued aggressively, and the use of chemical weapons such as

Agent Orange, which would cause countless problems for the US military in the many generations to come.

Broken Promises

Lyndon Johnson ran as the "peace" candidate in his 1964 campaign against Barry Goldwater, who wanted to escalate the military offensive against North Vietnam and the Viet Cong guerrillas. In October, at a campaign appearance in Ohio, Johnson promised that "we are not about to send American boys 9 or 10,000 miles away from home to do what Asian boys ought to be doing for themselves."

However, in the months ahead, Johnson would not live up to his promises as a presidential candidate. After the Gulf of Tonkin Resolution, Johnson rapidly increased the U.S. military presence in South Vietnam, adding 184,000 personnel by the end of 1965. The American people began to wonder. From 1965 through 1969, the Selective Service inducted an average of 300,000 young men per year, of which a considerable portion of American casualties came during that time period.

The U.S. military sprayed almost 20 million gallons of Agent Orange to defoliate the dense jungles of Vietnam in a campaign to deprive North Vietnam of its sanctuary. What many military leaders didn't realize was that Agent Orange contains a highly poisonous dioxin. Despite the passage of time, the U.S. government didn't acknowledge a connection between exposure to that dioxin and health problems faced by returning veterans such as Cliff Riley.

“The dioxin was making a lot of us sick,” said Riley, who was now president of the Buckeye State Council Vietnam Veterans of America. “If you looked at the veterans who were exposed to dioxin, they have a higher chance of getting various diseases such as Prostrate cancer, along with 16 other diseases.” Riley had two heart attacks by the time he was 40. His wife had a miscarriage. As time carried on, he had a kidney failure along with gallbladder problems. Riley was also diagnosed with colon cancer, and he now has diabetes. Much to Riley’s chagrin, his son was born with dyslexia and hip dysplasia, among other conditions. Only with the passage of the Agent Orange Act in 1991 did the government begin acknowledging and compensating veterans for illnesses related to dioxin exposure (Kimball, 2015).

In South Vietnam, issues with Agent Orange are ten times worse for the Vietnamese because they are living with it in their grounds and in their water supply. The whole country is saturated with dioxin. The populace has a higher cancer rate and more birth defects than we do.

Vietnam Syndrome

The horrors of the war and the U.S. military defeat were so traumatizing that some Americans believed that their country suffered from a "Vietnam Syndrome." The thought process behind the entire concept was that, because the Vietnam conflict had failed and been so unpopular among Americans, leaders are now very reluctant to use force overseas, says Edward Molter, a professor of History at Dartmouth University.

However, not everyone sees the Vietnam Conflict as a complete tragedy. As a country, we have the limits of American military power. The Bush administration took a significant lesson from Vietnam. Despite lessons learned, Vietnam remains a focus of much debate. Molter went on to explain further. "Whenever there is a debate about what the U.S. should do in Iraq or Afghanistan or with ISIS or anything like that, Vietnam is always the focal point that politicians and military leaders refer to first."

Many younger draft-age civilians accused the government of lying during the Vietnam era. As the U.S. escalated, many young people, such as Ken Williamson, began expressing themselves more openly. Despite his anger, Mr. Williamson decided to fulfill his obligation to his country. He initially received a deferment to fulfill his studies. Despite students' objections, the government did not change its course. Many students were concerned about their fate after graduation.

Williamson finally spoke out, “We’re involved in a civil war in Vietnam that I didn’t think we had any business being there for.” Unfortunately, after graduation, Williamson did a stint as a civilian employee at the Defense Intelligence Agency. Much to his chagrin, Williamson ran out of options and was eventually drafted. He was drafted into the US Army in 1968 and assigned as a photographer to document the work of military engineers as they built infrastructure in South Vietnam. Despite his negative feelings toward the country’s leaders, Williamson felt he had an obligation to serve.

Training

The general purpose of basic training (boot camp) during the Vietnam era was to take civilians - many of whom didn't actually want to be there - and turn them into soldiers in a very short period of time so they could be sent off to assist in the conflict, whether or not they were truly ready. This entire process included hardening these recruits and exposing them to conditions that may reflect what was happening during the war. This whole affair was mind-numbing to many recruits, and because of their inability to adjust, they were either wounded or lost their life.

According to Vietnam Veteran Charles A. Wells, Jr., many unforeseen realities made basic training very harsh. "For some mysterious reason, the designers of boot camp decided that we should be exposed to tear gas during week three of the cycle. I don't know if they thought we might develop a level of paranoia by breathing the fumes or just create a negative spirit after breathing in the fumes."

Training for deployment to Vietnam took into account a variety of factors, depending on the unit's specialization to which the individual service member was assigned. Training took place in the US, the Philippines, and other Pacific locations before deployment to South Vietnam. Much training changed over the course of the war in many different aspects. It all started with basic training, more commonly known as boot camp. Enlistees and draftees reported to their first military training station as low-ranking troops, where they were introduced to their drill instructor, who supervised their transition from civilians to soldiers, sailors, airmen, or marines.

The transition from civilian to servicemember was a culture shock for most new enlistees or draftees. This included appearances, starting with a new haircut, the transition from civilian clothes to military uniforms, and the use of military-issued toiletries. All civilian personal possessions were taken and packed away until the completion of boot camp.

The new enlistee quickly learned that the items they had known all their lives as one thing were given another name in whichever branch of the service they found themselves. Hats were no longer hats; they were covers. Sailors used a head when in search of a latrine. Marines received load-bearing equipment. Marching occupied most of the time in boot camp to teach discipline. Recruits marched in formation to meals, classes, exercises, lectures, training, and virtually every other activity designated to indoctrinate them into the armed forces during the eight or nine weeks' stay in basic training.

In conclusion, basic training came first in preparing a soldier for Vietnam. It started with basic combat training. From there, you could pursue specialized training in your career field, also known as your MOS (military occupational skill), or attend OCS (Officer Candidate School) to master military leadership skills. In basic training, the individual soldier will learn teamwork and discipline along with handling a weapon such as an M-16 (rifle) and a bayonet. The work is physically and mentally demanding. You'll experience stress, and the individual troop will test their limits. The individual soldier learns to trust their limits, know what to expect, and arrive prepared.

Officially, the basic training program during the Vietnam conflict called for 352 total hours of instruction, which equated to 44 hours a week for eight weeks. However, trainees who underwent the program recall the physical and emotional challenges. The lessons learned accounted for far more as war and life moved forward. Memories of basic training followed many veterans forward.

Basic training was followed by another eight weeks of advanced individual training (AIT) before recruits were shipped off to the front line. This was quite an experience for many young service members. AIT reinforced the instruction that was taught in basic with the addition of Land Navigation, additional training in small arms with chemical weapons, along with the necessary skills that were needed to maintain and fire coax weapons such as the M-60 machine gun and .50 caliber coax from a mounted position, such as an M-60 tank or a runabout.

Nearly every time recruits went to jog, march, camp, or perform drills, they did so at double time and in full gear. That included a uniform, boots, a pack, and a rifle. The whole purpose was to introduce real-world challenges and prepare soldiers for the front line. Veteran Larry Lettir recalled that, during specific exercises, trainers were expected to complete them in full gear.

The mile run was accomplished in combat boots, a steel pot, a rifle, and full field gear according to the Physical Readiness Training Field Manual. For recruits who may not have been used to getting up at the crack of dawn, they had no choice but to adapt. Veteran Jerry Prater recalled the following: “Our drill sergeants then informed us of several aspects of Army life, which were what we could expect while we were in basic training. Reveille (Bugle call) would be at 0500 every morning. We must rouse and get ready for the day and be in platoon formation outside of the barracks no later than 0530.”

Every basic training company had a company commander. The company commander or one of two training officers would inspect the four barracks each morning after the company had left for its training session. Once recruits had been roused for the morning, the first item on the agenda was not chow in the mess hall or a cup of coffee. They had to lace up their boots and hit the ground running, whether it be cleaning the barracks or physical training.

According to Vietnam Veteran Salvatore Di Blasio, “A normal day consisted of an early rise, probably with a morning run of about five or six miles, and then you were allowed to have breakfast”. Despite the amount of running that the individual troop completed before the sun rose over the horizon, there was always more to come. Training to be a hero was not always an easy thing to do.

Running wasn’t the only exercise or endurance test faced before reaching the mess hall. In some training sessions, troops had to deal with the horizontal ladder. Recruits were forced to repeatedly cross the horizontal ladder, known as the monkey bars, before every meal. This was designed to help build coordination and upper-body strength. This really strained almost every recruit's physical abilities.

In between the hours upon hours of physical training, recruits were also taught the basic lessons essential for serving in the armed forces. Classroom training included lessons on conduct, necessary medical knowledge, military courtesy, and the Uniform Code of

Military Justice. The education apparently didn't include much preparation for spending several years in Vietnam.

Vietnam veteran Mike Page recalled that the Army was trying to economize on training recruits. Individual training was very conservative, as if the military were more concerned with saving money than with properly training troops. That did not invest heavily in giving troops a real chance to survive once they arrived in Vietnam. Perhaps that training issue could have saved many young lives that had to go to Southeast Asia. Consequently, there was little formal training to prepare recruits to deal with the realities of the conflict. The bottom line is that the recruit shipping out to Vietnam was ill-prepared to fulfill their mission.

Nearly every day, recruits had to march out to the firing range, which at some installations was very far from the rest of the training sites. Sometimes the ranges were on the beach, and on many occasions the troops had to establish a bivouac site at the training grounds. According to Dennis Mulgannon, who was in the Special Forces during the Vietnam Conflict, they often trained with models they didn't end up using, "By the time I got to Vietnam, most of the bugs had been worked out of the M-16, but the problem was not with the weapon itself, in my opinion. The problem was that everyone had zero experience."

All the soldiers in the Vietnam Era were experts and knew how to master the M-14 because that was what every soldier trained in boot camp. However, that is a far different animal than the weapon actually being used on the war front. Many troops could strip and reassemble the M-14 blindfolded, but most had never had formal hands-on training with the M-16.

A block of time totaling about eight hours was dedicated to teaching recruits hand-to-hand combat, essentially to build confidence when close-quarter fighting was called for. This included grappling, pugil stick, and bayonet training. This has largely been replaced by calisthenics and other forms of physical training. Combat training was a significant part of the drills for recruits during the Vietnam War. According to Vietnam Veteran Fred Childs, "the drill instructors really hammered home the importance of becoming skilled, efficient in these forms of hand-to-hand combat.

The actual amount of physical training was staggering for recruits, and the confidence built by the obstacle courses was among the most challenging parts of that training. The obstacle courses included overhead bars, wall climbs, rope climbing among other challenges. Adverse weather also took its toll on recruits during this type of training. Vietnam veteran Charles A. Wells Jr. noted, "My least favorite event was the low crawl under strands of barbed wire for fifty yards with intermittent bursts of machine gun fire overhead."

Not only did training create artificial stress, but the chow hall did as well. When it came to eating, recruits didn't have much leeway to think for themselves. They had to follow a specific procedure and protocol to enter the mess hall, and while they were eating, drill instructors would scream at them to eat faster, as if the recruits were almost inhaling the food. It was even worse for the trainees who had to perform kitchen police (KP) duties.

Vietnam Veteran, Jerry Prattee, recalled his time at Fort Polk, "All of the trainees would be required to serve KP at any point in the training. Those assigned to pull KP on any given week would be awakened at approximately 0430 so they could get dressed and report to the mess hall to assist with breakfast preparation. The details required for enlisted personnel to assist with breakfast preparation. They would continue with the detail until after the dinner meal and the mess hall had been policed. The grease trap was a never-ending issue.

It's no coincidence that what people think of the Vietnam era and drill sergeants is shaped by R. Lee Ermey's performance as Gunnery Sergeant Hartman in Full Metal Jacket. Ermey served as a drill instructor during the Vietnam Era and brought his experience to the forefront when playing this notorious character. In reality, drill instructors were quite boisterous with recruits until they started performing like fully matured soldiers.

The drill instructors were in everyone's face at one time or another. Without hesitation, they did their best to dominate and to terrorize an individual recruit, which is what they were employed to do. They ruled their platoons by terror on any given day. It was their job to take you apart and rebuild you the Army way, mentally. Once they realized you were in the program, they left you alone and focused on your needs for focus and motivation.

After a long day, recruits often struggled to get a decent night's rest because the training was more than most could endure. Also, their nights were interrupted when the recruits were expected to pull fire guard. According to many Vietnam veterans, drill instructors at various installations were noted for saying that even a smoldering butt could cause a great deal of damage if it weren't detected. A barracks would have been down in 17 minutes if there had not been an alert fire guard paying attention. Without hesitation, a handful of trainees picked by the drill instructor had to perform fire guard on one-hour shifts.

To prevent or detect a fire as soon as it starts, recruits would be required to conduct a fire watch from 2100 to 0500 on both floors of the barracks. A trainee on each floor would be assigned in full fatigues to walk up and down the barracks and be alert to any potential fire hazards.

Post-traumatic stress disorder (PTSD)

American service members have struggled with the issues of PTSD for almost four decades from Vietnam forward (Tull, 2020). Our understanding of PTSD has grown by leaps and bounds in the medical community. Once referred to by terms such as "shell shock," the full impact of this diagnosis has become much clearer in the decades following the Vietnam Conflict. It has been a new challenge for veterans who are obligated to seek treatment in the mental health community.

PTSD is also a mental health condition that can be triggered by a terrifying event, either experiencing it or witnessing it. Symptoms may include flashbacks, nightmares, or severe anxiety, as well as uncontrollable thoughts. The ultimate consideration regarding PTSD is to recognize the negative impact it can have on a person's daily life. The Vietnam War is not over for any person who has been diagnosed with PTSD because of it. That person must keep moving forward to survive. For many servicemembers, the war is yet to be over, but healing is still occurring every day for many of these heroes.

Author's notes:

I must have believed myself to be relatively impervious when I was in the military as a company-grade officer until after I experienced a traumatic brain injury for the first time in my life. I never knew what PTSD was either until I had to report back to duty the following morning.

I never anticipated my car wreck on the autoroute that cold and rainy night, but then again, in my wildest dreams, did I know that I was suffering from PTSD, among other illnesses? To fool myself, I thought I was the man, the myth, the fighting machine until that unforgettable moment. I never really took the time to realize how immature a fool I was. I constantly damn myself for not being more aware of my own weaknesses.

Air Cav 101
Based on an Interview with Lt. Jay Snyder

This was a tough period for me. I thought it was exciting that you referred to the period as "growing pains," which really could describe a lot of what each of us experienced in college. There was very little difference in my attitude towards Vietnam. Vietnam was pretty much a non-issue where I went to school. There were just over 600 students when I started in 1960, and by the time I graduated in 1964, there were still fewer than 1000 students.

I was an English and theater major with a history minor. During my junior year, I took a two-semester course in Far Eastern history. This was my first real exposure to French Indochina. The two textbook chapters on the country discussed the former monarchy and the ongoing wars with China. There were discussions about the end of World War II and the French occupation. This is how the world dealt with its problems.

I later learned about US involvement, which seemed to be peripheral: we supported the French with money and weapons. After Dien Bien Phu, as the French withdrew, we were banned from helping the sitting government against the Viet Minh, but that was advisors (the first boots on the ground and some money). I remember almost none of that from college, but I did read “Street without Joy” by Bernard Fall on the ship while sailing to Vietnam.

Fifteen months later, while stationed at Ft Bragg, my roommate's post was a Special Forces Capt. And he had studied quite a bit about Vietnam. He had been invited there in 620-63 and even had been wounded before Purple Hearts were authorized for VN service. He had written two Master’s Theses about Vietnam, one focusing on the Montagnards and the other on the gradual changes in government. We had many conversations, which prompted me to continue studying about Vietnam until I had accumulated close to 100 books about the country and the war.

I have visited the French version of our Vietnam Veterans Memorial half a dozen times. It is just outside Frejus in the north. The monument differs from Mars in several ways. First, it is considerably larger, covering more than ten acres. Second, it honors the following about the Algerian and Indochinese 02 campaigns. Third, more than a thousand of those who have died in the conflict are actually buried in the monument. There is also a small museum on site, and finally, hardly anyone visits. In contrast, the wall in DC is still among the most visible spots in Washington.

I felt a bit apprehensive, but mostly excited and eager. Knowing what I do now, those emotions were pretty misplaced. But from the moment I knew I was headed to Southeast Asia, I was very confident I would survive...I never doubted that I would not die in combat. As I sadly learned, many, many of my fellow soldiers who thought they would die, did.

For example, my second company commander had even gone so far as to send instructions home for planning his funeral, including music selections and the choice of pallbearers. He was killed three months after he assumed command of our company. One of my platoon members expressed to me several times that he knew he would be killed by artillery.

He was always terrified, and as well as he could, he hid every time I called in artillery. Just after I left the platoon, he was killed by one of our own short HE rounds. I still visit his grave a couple of times a year in Bainbridge, just down the Susquehanna from my hometown. I'm sure you have all the stories about the most dangerous periods of time for a combat infantryman. The first month he is in country and the last. The first is that he doesn't know what he is doing (especially true in Vietnam, when 90% of the infantrymen arrived as replacements for units that had not experienced combat).

The FNG was always the most at risk, and the best always worked carefully around them. The last month was risky because you knew when you were going home, and you started to be extra, changing the routine that had kept you alive to date. My platoon sergeant was killed a few weeks before he was scheduled to go home, as were two of my platoon members. That was way more than you asked, but as I started answering the questions of war, this is what related to me.

Just before I graduated from college in 1964, I learned from the daughter of the head of my county draft board that I would be number one on the draft list for that July, so I started exploring options for enlisting. To make a much longer story short, the Army had just put in place the new "College Option" program – if you were a college graduate, you would be guaranteed OCS. I chose that option and was in the first class. My fellow College OP classmates and I completed basic training and AIT at Fort Gordon.

After a short Christmas/New Year's leave, we entered OCS on 10 January, class 6-65. Over a third of my classmates did not finish. I was among those who did (at that time, there were only classes in infantry and artillery). In a few short months, many other branch options would open as the infantry and artillery would ramp up. Now, OCS is the "branch immaterial" and requires college graduation. After graduation and jump school, I was assigned to the First Cav.

My own basic training in 1964 prepared me to be a soldier, but did little to prepare me for Vietnam. There were only passing moments to reflect on the upcoming war, and the only weapons we trained with were M-14s, which included marksmanship, bayonet, and grenade-throwing training. I did use the training and practice in grenade throwing to good effect in Vietnam, but never touched an M-14 after OCS.

The most valuable training I got in AIT was learning to spot well-camouflaged enemies and booby traps. That class has stayed with me all my life and proved exceptionally valuable in Vietnam. We had never had any type of jungle warfare training before OCS. Some classes would have been invaluable if they had been adapted to a jungle environment. Unfortunately, we were never out of the jungle, and we were at a loss on many days.

Discipline, the phonetic alphabet, standing orders, the Geneva Convention, and radio procedures all proved valuable at one time or another in Vietnam, but didn't readily prepare me for combat. Map reading, use of maps for calling in artillery fire support. However, the best combat training was OJT.

I was able to train with my men for 2 months before we left by troopship from Savannah for South Vietnam. Those of us who have survived have reconnected since around 2000 and have begun holding annual reunions. We are down to about 40 remaining from our original company, including myself and only one other officer. It turns out the OCS class had the most KIAs of any class in Vietnam and was also the most decorated, including two Medal of Honor Winners.

Not surprising since just about all of us were in Vietnam within a few months of graduation. I never considered any branch other than infantry and had always planned to enlist in the Army. My grandfather enlisted in the Army in WWI; my mother's brother was in the Army in WWII; and my father's sister was in WWI as a WAC. I don't believe I know of any relatives who were in other branches, so it was in my blood, I guess. Except for the draft, which swelled the military ranks for about 7 years, there have not been many volunteers. As I understand, less than 2 percent of the population made the effort.

Training was very difficult for the air cavalry units. It might surprise you to know that the training to prepare for cavalry deployment was heavily focused on logistics. My unit was already battle-tested. Most of my unit had been in the Dominican Republic and had been training together for quite a long time as part of the

11th. The 11th was the experimental unit tasked with demonstrating the efficiency of helicopter-based warfare.

The creation of the new cavalry was the result of a decision in June 1965. The colors of the cavalry were brought back from Korea and, in a very elaborate ceremony, were exchanged for the Benny base colors of the second infantry division; soon thereafter, the cavalry became the first Airborne brigade. The remainder of the cavalry was what had been the 2nd. In the two months I was with them before we had one brief war game exercise against parts of the 101st. The rest of the time was spent preparing for the jungle by getting new fatigues and awaiting new weapons. The time on the ship was devoted to a battalion-wide competition to determine which of the three battalions would be the first to land on the beaches in South Vietnam. My own Charlie Co. won without question, with my own favorite platoon leading the way.

Helicopters were new to us, considering we were the Air Cav. Our early helicopters were UH-14 and Chinooks. There were also Eastern teams for observation during our first major deployment, when medevacs refused to lay in, and one of the 13-year-old pilots began taking wounded now to have time, just like in M.A.S.H. Cobras came along after several months, as did the giant sky cranes. Huey's were pretty basic, all with the doors and only minimal old seating.

The helicopters were all based on what became known as the golf course. I always thought it was so named because courses rang it. Turns out it was because we were creating the base, which came the way the division wanted the pad for the helicopters to use.

The base camp started as hundreds of shelter halves, each housing two troopers. It seemed to grow daily. In any case, barracks-sized tents seem to arrive daily and are erected one at a time in each company area. Other types of tents were also delivered and erected. The advance party had clearly staked out plans for what was to go where and when everybody arrived. Some of the plans were washed away in the heavy rain. The first communal part of the camp was centered around the latrines.

A battalion aid station was built near the headquarters tent. Next was a large barracks tent dubbed "the enlisted members club," followed a week later by a similar-looking NCO club. We gradually built an officer's club from ammo boxes. We had our grand opening in about six weeks, with pink champagne and four bottles of Kahlua. This was quite an accomplishment for something that had no organization.

I clearly remember the mud, which was everywhere thanks to the monsoons. In the central highlights, you had to live with the southernmost monsoons. Then, some weeks later, the northern monsoons became an issue. Roasting cans were almost impassable thanks to some vehicles. We were able to bypass many roads by driving mules with four small, flatbed four-wheelers. If you could envision a large floor with four wheels, that would be the mule, and you could go almost anywhere with a massive payload.

The camp was initially surrounded by two or three courses of concertina wire. Just outside the wire was the trash and garbage, so this was another spot that steadily grew. Civilians were constantly picking over this spot. Worker parties made up of Vietnamese civilians cleared brush and trees six days a week. Unlike some other military installations in the country, we didn't have civilian workers on base. Each time we returned from the field, we noticed noticeable changes at the base camp, which looked more like a permanent base.

The cavalry in the 60s was different from today's; virtually everyone was infantry. The first, second, and third brigades each had three battalions, each with all troopers holding the infantry MOS. All those in the first brigade were airborne infantry (after 16 months, the Cav decided it no longer needed an airborne capability; however, those troopers on jump status got to make jump pays over 3 months). We jumped from Hueys and quickly turned into clay pigeons. The VC quickly realized they could take potshots at these free-hanging targets. Thankfully, the VC were lousy shots, and none of the troopers in our company got hurt.

Our central full-scale mission started on October 12, 1965. Companies A and B air assaulted into the Suoi la Thinh River Valley. My platoon, along with the rest of Charlie Co., attacked into the S'suoi Ca Dinh Valley up into the mountain on a search and destroy mission. Over the next several days, we found and destroyed large amounts of rice that had been provided to the VC by villages below, which were surrounded by productive rice paddies. The VC demanded rice as a kind of tax from the villages. At first, we burned the piles of rice, and then we arranged to have the last few piles flown into the South Vietnamese Army. We also found a cache of hidden weapons. We had minimal enemy contact and suffered no casualties. After about a week, we began to work our way into the valley for extraction.

Shortly after we landed on day one of our mission, we could hear explosions and small-arms fire in the distance as A and B companies engaged what we later learned was a reinforced VC battalion. They suffered many casualties, and the engagement earned the battalion decorations: our battalion, Capt. Billy Lord had carried several wounded men to safety during the battle and arranged for their evacuation. After the first medevac helicopter took heavy fire, others refused to land to continue picking up wounded.

With the medevacs facing difficulties, the battalion XO, Joe Belochi (also a pilot), was flying his H13 observation helicopter and directing artillery fire. Hearing the radio traffic and learning what had stopped the evacuation of the wounded, he proceeded to land, pick up the wounded troopers, and fly them back to the battalion aid station. He returned three more times, under fire, and evacuated the remaining wounded. He later received the Distinguished Flying Cross for his actions, and Captain Lord received the Silver Star.

Back to Charlie Company, we set up in the dry paddies to await extraction in the morning. A reporter, Charlie Black from the Columbus Enquirer, who had accompanied us on the ship to Vietnam, had been with my platoon for three straight days of the week we were out. While he and I were talking quietly, it began to rain hard. Several hours later, we awoke to steadily rising water in the paddy, which left us open to long green leeches. We all learned on the spot how to get leeches off our bodies without matches. You need to put salt on them or spray them with insect repellent. When it was daylight, a lit cigarette did the trick, but in rainy conditions, light discipline resorted to more extreme methods.

After our first real mission in enemy combat, we returned to base camp for cleanup and refitting. During the next-to-last week in October, the Ple Me special forces camp west of Pleiku came under heavy VC attack. The first brigade was airlifted into the area of operation. "All the way began the first part of what became the Pleiku Campaign." Later made famous in the Mel Gibson movie "We Were Soldiers Once and Young". We moved northwest toward Plei Me in sufficient strength so that the VC, who would point to ambush whatever you did that came to the aid of the surrounded camp, thought better of it and headed toward the Cambodian border. We spent the next 18 days clearing small pockets of resistance all the way to the Chu Phong Massif and the Cambodian border. We captured numerous weapons, including crew-served and automatic weapons, as well as extensive communication equipment. We had sporadic contact but only a few casualties. Malaria reared its ugly head, and a few men had to be medevacked.

One evening, I sent out an ambush control which made a heavy contact with a group of VC moving along a trail about 1 AM. My team leader had been seriously wounded by an enemy grenade, which he had picked up and thrown back toward the VC. It detonated a few feet from him, causing shrapnel wounds to his head and chest. His right eye had been damaged. I took three of my men and my radio operator, and we quietly headed down the trail to bring back the wounded. This was my first, but not my last, brush with fear. It was pitch black, and my imagination made every bush into an enemy soldier. I had called medevac, and it arrived shortly. We loaded the most seriously wounded men on board, and the chopper lifted off.

This was the last anyone saw of my team leader for more than 30 years. Sadly, this was standard operating procedure. Once, a man was seriously wounded and was medevacked; you not only never saw them again, but you never heard if they survived. A couple of days later, we were moving carefully because we were clearly in enemy territory when my point man called a halt and asked me to join him. He had come across a wire with a frame right and left across the trail that we were moving on. This was a clear indication of VC. I put outflank security and stayed with the point man. We moved even more slowly and expected more danger.

I had never thought I would have a second fear, frankly. We expected to be hit at almost any time. Unknowingly, there were a few stances of blue sweatshirts, enough for each member of my team to have one. There were stacks of canvas rucksacks, also sufficient for anyone to take one. In fact, I used the VC rucksack for the rest of my time in Vietnam. It was lighter, more comfortable, and held more than the Army-issued one.

During the Pleiku campaign, known to most as the Battle of the Ia Drang Valley, our first, second, and third brigades killed more than 3500 NV soldiers from the 32nd, 33rd, and 66th NVA regiments. In fact, the 32nd was nearly obliterated. The Cav also took almost 157 prisoners. Some carried valuable intelligence information, and more than 900 individuals and 126 crew-served weapons with enough ammunition to arm an NVA battalion were also captured.

Mid-December saw the beginning of Operation Clean House, focusing on the opposite direction – to the east of our base camp. Back to the Soul Ca Valley again and beyond. We would be picked up, landed in a new LZ, and would move, almost away in platoon-size groups, clearly in the valleys – normally paddy-filled and then into the jungle to hillsides. We could cover a lot of territory in valleys, but it was slow to a crawl as we hacked our way through dense jungles.

A couple of experiences really stand out in my memory. The first was moving along a broad, shallow, rock-filled river when, suddenly, we were attacked by hundreds of chattering, moving monkeys. It was almost as if we were walking on a slow river of water with monkeys above us. We could barely hear ourselves think at that point. I got us out of that chatter as quickly as possible. We were grateful for the lack of noise.

The second experience underscored for me was the extreme jungle beauty of Vietnam. Several days later, we were moving along a stream when it suddenly widened and became extremely shallow. We moved out into the water, which would make it easier to proceed and leave no trace of our presence. We had covered perhaps 350 to 400 meters when my point man stopped and motioned for me to move forward. We were stunned to be standing at the top of a 50meter high and vast waterfall, the first of its kind that we had seen in Vietnam, and it was the most beautiful scene.

Of course, we were very exposed, so we put out our flank security and continued on our forward mission into the valley below. I left part of my platoon on flank security. Eventually, we found a small trail we had passed while working our way into the water. With my squad and my radio operator, I slowly headed down the trail to the cool, very green, lush areas around the falls. For some reason, the scene reminded me of an old Tarzan movie, and in those old movies, there was always a cave behind the falls, so I asked two of my men to explore it.

Sure enough, came a cry from one of my men, “You ain’t going to believe this”. We made our way very carefully behind the falls, and there was indeed a cave, vast and damp and easy enough to stand in. It was tough to determine how far back the cave extended. The area where we stood was littered with small animal bones.

There were also the remains of an ancient campfire. Everything was extremely damp, with mold growing on the cave's wet walls.

There was no evidence, besides the old fire, that anyone had been there. We didn't have a flashlight, so we could not explore more than ten or fifteen feet back into the cave. I reluctantly left and headed back up the trail (after filling all our canteens with the clear pool water and dropping in two halazone tablets to purify and destroy the taste). It was getting late, so we established a perimeter near the head of the falls. I sent out 3-man ambush patrols, spaced about 50 meters on either side of the stream. Negative contact and mid-morning, we were air-lifted out to head elsewhere. The best LZ was the open, shallow stream. This was the only time we were airlifted out to head elsewhere, where the airlift did not generate a wash.

Our next mission was to help open and secure Highway 19, which connected Qui Nhon and Pleiku. Our base camp was roughly halfway. So, we now have our first experience with convoy security. We joined the truck convoy at A Khe, and I was in a jeep while my men were deployed throughout a section of the larger convoy. The VC had gotten around to using landmines on the road, but there was always the danger of an ambush at Pang Yang Pass.

Many things have changed since my time in Vietnam. I am not alone, but I am alone with thoughts. Sharing this has been a real challenge, and I welcome it openly. Carl expressed his thoughts while I rambled on, but I am sure he will take time out to make his thoughts welcome. Jay… it was an honor to work with you on this project. Unfortunately, because of the pandemic, I didn't get the whole truth, but what you shared with me was incredible. I could imagine the energy you put into protecting your troops and fulfilling the mission. If our paths ever cross again, just think that I think of you as a true American hero and that your call to duty will be remembered by the people who read this.

I came back to the US from Vietnam via a medical evacuation. I had developed an infection after returning to the field from my hospitalization after being wounded in late May, and rather than send me to Japan, I had less than a month on my 12-month tour. They decided to send me to Valley Forge Military Hospital, a suburban Philadelphia hospital. I left on a litter from the 85th Evac Hospital in Qui Nhon, exactly where we had landed ten months earlier. The ambulance I was in hit a civilian while on the way to the airport, and I had to be transferred to another ambulance.

We flew to Clark Air Base in the Philippines, where I spent about a week before flying on to Guam for refueling, then on to Hawaii, where we were allowed off the plane for a few hours. I took advantage of the time to buy a Coke and place a collect call to my family in PA.

Then on to Austin, TX, and from there to the airbase at Ft Dix, NJ. I was then transported by ambulance to Valley Forge, where I could finally shower and change into the blue hospital garments. My first order of business was to call the young co-ed who had been writing me the whole time I was in Vietnam; unfortunately, she was out, so I spoke with her mother. When she came home around 10, her mother told her that I had called, and she immediately called the hospital.

Unfortunately for her, the hospital would not accept any incoming phone calls after 9 pm. I got the message that she would be visiting as soon as possible, the next day. The next afternoon, she walked into my room with a nervous "Hi', and a little wave. You have to understand, we had been on this artificial courtship by mail for 9 months or so, and that included promises of a passionate welcome whenever.

At this point, we had never met, and it was the first time; it was a bit overwhelming. I was 5 years older than her, and she was about to be a college junior. No passion, just a feeling of exceptional attraction. She was much prettier in person than in any picture. For the first two weeks of my hospital stay, I wasn't allowed out at all, so we talked a couple of times a day on the phone. As an officer, I had a private room and telephone. When I was finally allowed out for a few hours, Jeanne picked me up, and we went to her house for dinner.

We saw each other almost daily for the rest of my stay till real life got in the way. Jeanne had to return, and I had received a call from the Pentagon offering me an excellent next assignment to return to duty for the next nine months as the Public Relations officer for the US Army Parachute Team, the Golden Knights at Fr Bragg, N.C.

I had a month's compassionate leave before reporting to Bragg, so I returned to my parents' home and got to making up for lost time, despite a bit of time lost with my old girlfriend. I realized that Jeanine was somebody special, and I started visiting her at school.

The relationship continued to blossom, as I eventually set up housekeeping with a Special Forces Captain (who advertised for a roommate to share apartment expenses). That took care of my accommodations. The Army was obviously counting on my staying on after my two-year obligation ended in June '67.

The Army had not reckoned on the influence of love. Except for the time the Knights were on the road, I was with them. I was spending almost two weekends a month driving to PA to see

Jeanne… leaving Friday after duty, driving all night, then returning Sunday afternoon and making it back in time to report in for duty Monday morning. Evenings were spent on the telephone talking to Jeanne.

In December, I asked her to marry me, and we began planning our life together. Initially, we planned for me to stay in the Army, but then we had other ideas. I was looking at another further tour in Vietnam, probably within a year, and most likely as an infantry company Commander. George, Jeanne's father, was pretty adamant that this was not what he expected for his daughter.

My priority by that time was Jeanne, not a military career. So, I announced my intent to leave the service in mid-June. Within several weeks, I had been reassigned to a training company as the Supply Officer. The message was obvious.

Unfortunately, I saw several negative issues. I ran into fewer of the other guys who returned from Vietnam after me. Remember, unlike many, returning Vets who were discharged after they got back faced some tough challenges and did not have the polish to succeed in the civilian community.

I had almost ten months left in uniform. So, during that time, aside from what I saw on TV, I encountered no discrimination or protests while stationed at Ft Bragg. I was discharged in late June of 1967, married in August, and moved into our first apartment outside Millersville.

My first job was in Harrisburg, and I commuted by train daily. My first truly negative experience came within a month of moving in. Our apartment was just outside town, and right up the road was the local VFW Post. So, I took a Saturday off and stopped by to join. It was not very clean, and I was not very welcome. In fact, one member said, "Come back and see us after you fight in a real war." Many vets had the same experience with the VFW and American Legion.

The attitude of the old school organizations led to the establishment of the Vietnam Veterans of America (VOA). Ironically, most of the older VSOs are not a part of the VOA. The VOA is doing its best to incorporate the new generation of veterans from Desert Storm and Afghanistan. Many years later, I was invited to the statewide VFW as an open member, and a lot of the negativities had been erased from 1967

I am now a proud life member of the VFW, the American Legion, the Disabled American Veterans, the Purple Heart Association, the Combat Infantrymen's, the National Sojourner's, the Vietnam Veterans of America, the First Cavalry Association, the 12th Cavalry, and the Central Pennsylvania Vietnam Roundtable.

Author's Note:

Since 1980, PTSD referred to as the "inability of a person to process trauma that may have resulted from exposure to war, physical or sexual violence, terrorism, or natural disasters" (Bauer, 2015). Clinicians are aware of how PTSD affects the patient, the spouse or partner, children, other family members, friends, the outside community in general, and the mental health community as a whole. There can be moral injury as a result of being exposed to PTSD. Trauma can affect how individuals interpret their spiritual, moral, or ethical understanding of the importance of being accepted within the human race and of having a personal relationship with God. In the foreseeable future, PTSD will continue to exist as a challenge to upcoming conflicts throughout the world.

Trauma Everlasting

According to medical journals, PTSD, or Post-Traumatic Stress Disorder, is a psychiatric disorder that can occur following an experience or witnessing a life-threatening event such as military combat, a natural disaster, a terroristic incident, a serious accident, or some type of physical or sexual assault. Most survivors of trauma return to normal a little bit at a time. However, when the trauma does not want to go away on its own, people may develop PTSD. People who suffer from PTSD often relive their experiences through nightmares and flashbacks, which cause them to overlook the simple things in life.

Physical wounds can be devastating or deadly. Psychological wounds are unseen, yet destroy thousands of warriors, and have for centuries. An article entitled "The Walking Wounded – PTSD from Ancient Greece to Afghanistan, "[1] outlines the history of PTSD through the ages. According to the article, throughout the 1960s and 1970s, tens of thousands of American combat veterans from the Vietnam War returned from the jungles of Southeast Asia suffering from a range of flashback symptoms that could be triggered by any source, or from other debilitating symptoms and mood disorders that could be attached to emotional issues. There were other physical manifestations, including headaches, chest pain, and dizziness. Compounding the ailments, neither the medical community nor the U.S. military was well equipped to handle the physical injuries that were being caused, let alone the psychological illnesses of survivors. Those psychological injuries were not overlooked; it was just not understood how deeply combat veterans were affected, especially by what is now known as PTSD.

The article emphasizes, however, that the U.S. forces in Southeast Asia were not the first combat veterans affected by PTSD. The ancient Greek historian Herodotus may have been one of the first to write about the emotional strain of war. In his account of the Battle of Marathon in 490 BC, he noted a stressor similar to PTSD in one veteran who had struggled in combat. Known only to his fellow warriors as Epizeluz, he was in an incredible battle by Greco-Roman standards, in which a force of 10,000 Greeks repelled a force of Persians almost twice its size. Epizeluz mysteriously lost his sight in a slight skirmish with a Persian, amongst the battlefield cluttered with nearly 200 dead Greeks and more than 6,000 dead Persians. Army physicians could find no wounds or abrasions on Epizeluz, and he had a difficult time explaining how he had lost his vision. It was thought that the combat brought on a case of hysterical blindness. He never regained his vision.

Centuries later, according to "The Walking Wounded," symptoms of PTSD became more evident due to the development of gunpowder and subsequent endless wars.

Austrian physician Josef Leopold

Auenbrugger, at the end of the Seven Years' War, observed symptoms in soldiers including depression, physical exhaustion, and angst. However, he blamed the source of the anxiety not on the horrors of war, but on homesickness. Likewise, Dr. Johannes Hofer, a Swiss physician, who noted a similar condition among his country's troops a century earlier, blamed homesickness, as did physicians in the Napoleonic era.

During the American Civil War, which claimed 600,000 lives and injured more than a million combatants, a surgeon named Jacob Mendez Da Costa completed a study of approximately 300 soldiers who complained of physical symptoms, fatigue, and chest pains. According to "The Walking Wounded," Dr. Da Costa and other doctors in the late 19th century saw the psychological stressors as being related to the physical stressors of wartime, along with sleep deprivation and carrying too much heavy equipment. In particular, the tremendous weight of the rucksack, along with the tight straps, led to damage in the upper torso region. With a slight modification, "Dr. Da Costa's Syndrome" was, in all likelihood, a manifestation of wartime elements that caused stress to a soldier's heart. "Soldier's

Heart" was finally reclassified as a psychological condition.

Science and technology made considerable advances by World War I, yet, according to "The Walking Wounded," even the brightest minds were clueless about the seeming darkness that plagued the armies on the Western Front. From the start, combat soldiers showed signs of anxiety, as well as dizziness and tremors, as a reaction to noise. These side effects were attributed to neurological damage and the emotional trauma activated by the horrors of trench warfare, poison gas, and the damage caused by being in 'No Man's Land.' Artillery bursts physically injured the brain, causing concussions and damage to the nervous system. This became known as "shell shock," and by the end of 1914, between 4 and ten percent of soldiers and officers had signs of it. By 1916, up to forty percent of all military combat injuries were associated with shell shock.

An article entitled "Battle Fatigue, Post-

Traumatic Stress Disorder, Combat Stress"[2]

discusses the way stress may present itself while a soldier or individual is engulfed in hostile action combative, to say the least.

A hero may suffer from military action or a civilian accident without obtaining any physical injuries. Battlefield stress corresponds to the phenomenon of anxiety, which is an issue in the civilian world that is brought about by serious problems such as witnessing or experiencing violence, lost jobs, or other issues affecting people's personal lives. There are well-established treatment plans that are available to reduce or resolve the inner trials and tribulations associated with anxiety.

The article describes how forms of mental relaxation, such as deep breathing and muscle relaxation, make it easier to focus on simple routines. Dealing with anxiety at this level provides for re-found humor that may help in dealing with unseen anxiety. Severe forms of anxiety require a more intense exploration of relaxation, potentially with medication.

As pointed out by "Battle Fatigue," the injured person suffers not only from the sickening condition of anxiety but also from insecurity and is potentially incapable of handling future life situations. The person may be faced with the growing fear of a possible mental illness, such as PTSD or concussion syndrome. An individual needs to be reassured that their anxieties can be cured, and that they won't need to crawl into some black hole of traumatic fear if not appropriately treated. The person dealing with a negative outlook must show a high degree of discipline to survive the struggle by not giving in to anxiety. Patience must be learned with every step one takes. It may take years for all the issues and symptoms to dissipate.

Anxiety can be viewed as a common discomfort for almost all people who experience any mental or physical pain associated with illness. According to "Battle Fatigue," a competent psychiatrist or psychologist can offer appropriate recommendations to treat anxiety, keeping in mind the fact that the recommendations may not be completely fulfilling. Individuals challenged with anxiety need to retain their own confidence, because while overcoming anxiety can be awkward and demanding, it can be accomplished. The effect of anxiety is temporary.

"Battle Fatigue" describes how a veteran may experience a psychological vacuum after the war. The intensity of the team environment is lost, often leading to a sense of negativity towards the veteran's survival. When the veteran's life becomes full of disparity after this psychological breakdown, it may also lead to difficulties with family and marriage. Many veterans returning from war may have joined the armed forces merely to fulfill the identity of belonging to a military community. In that environment, they were required to satisfy the differences and realities of their lives in ways they had never done before. These were challenges that a civilian community may never be able to fulfill. As veterans, many feel there are inadequate job placement services, educational opportunities, such as college acceptance, and access to other helpful programs, such as internships with local agencies or community services. The abilities and needs of many veterans are often not correctly anticipated, which compounds the effects of trauma.

PTSD. I don't think anyone realized how much I hated the word or how warped I had become because of it. I bow my head in silence at this point, seeking some type of relief from the mental pain that was triggered within me almost every night. What many don't realize is that PTSD has no friends; it is a silent evil waiting to strike at nearly any moment. It has no honesty to it. PTSD triggers unwanted and intense moments of trauma.

Thoughts from yesteryear would plague me to no end almost every night. I remember the burn site in Iraq and members of my platoon just screaming out in agony. The flashbacks would not go away. I seemed unable to live in reality. My negative feelings ran wild for no reason. Why I put myself through this, I will never know. I didn't deserve this, and no one else did either. The memories of combat, the memories of death and killing would never fade away. I felt like my life was going to be a disaster. I begged for peace of mind, but that peace was beyond my grasp. I just wanted to have the anger within myself disappear. I could not focus on anything positive that would move me forward. Would my life ever be the same, I wondered?

I sat in total silence, begging for peace of mind. It was too much. Life as I knew it was about to change, but I didn't know in what direction. Coldness burned within my heart. I had never experienced anger to this degree before. I had let my platoon down, and I had let myself down as a leader. I didn't know if I had the individual strength to move beyond that nightmare, much less deal with the pitfalls of PTSD, and to make matters worse, I had no balance in my life. This was a journey I had to brave on my own.

When the Army first led me down this path to make a leader of men out of me, I couldn't imagine how arduous this journey would be and the struggles that would bring me back stateside to Walter Reed. I thought it would be easier to end it all right then and there, but for some reason, I knew I could not quit on myself. I didn't see myself as a coward desiring to cheat myself out of any attempt to have complete normalcy: PTSD or no PTSD. I just wanted one chance at true normalcy, true honesty.

One thing that seemed to defy me from the get-go was a positive reaction to the real world after I started having issues with Post-Traumatic Stress Disorder. I could not seem to leave behind the endless voyage or trauma that plagued me. I didn't know if I could outgrow the issues that haunted me--I had bought into an endless cycle of fear at Walter Reed. Life was not true to me at that point.

I began to dream, but I was afraid to let myself go. I was scared of being lost within my troubles once again. I was scared to relive yesterday's memories. To relive the negativity was a truly horrific experience, and the triggers that made my thoughts so horrifying in nature. Damn the experience that made my life into such a terrible moment. My mental energies were being wasted, and I could not escape the trauma. I begged God to spare me the emotions of having to endure so much negative energy and snap me out of the oblivion I was in.

I was always afraid of the twilight ever since I had to start dealing with trauma. As the thunder rolled in over the hospital, I knew this was going to be no exception. My psychiatrist had advised me to avoid many things, but being strapped to a hospital bed would not allow me to do so, no matter how much I wanted to follow his advice. Something so meaningless to others was terribly dangerous to me. I was so gullible at this point as to why it was so harmful to me, but I could not escape what I had no chance against. No matter how hard I tried, I could not hide away from the trauma that had been imposed upon me by the rigors of war.

I don't know why I thought that such a simplistic thing could occupy my thoughts, but I asked the orderly for a piece of fruit to help me occupy my focus from the nightmare that had just flashed before my eyes. My mind was so weak at this point that I thought this little distraction would help me return to enjoying reality with the rest of the world. I was such a fool to believe that I could guide my own rehabilitation. I took one bite of the fruit, and within seconds, I spit it out. The fruit tasted like sand, and I thought the orderly was playing tricks on me. My nostrils flared, looking for a fight, but I was too weak even to expect that of myself. At that moment, another orderly entered the room because he had heard the commotion. I was confused. I didn't want to face the truth, an endless cycle of traumatic insights.

One of the orderlies tried to calm my nerves as the other one cleaned up the mess from my disruptive behavior. The orderly explained to me that this was probably just a small example of how triggers worked. This was no fault of my own. I couldn't help but swear at myself, damning a moment of truth and wondering if this self-imposed devastation would ever disappear or if there would be an easy answer to help me adjust. I was mentally exhausted and afraid to let the evening take me away from trouble. The psychiatric nurse just popped his head into my room and smiled to reassure me. I could barely muster a greeting. I had the deepest fear of what my sleep would be like. I knew the nightmares of the past were still there, and I was unsure of my ability to handle them properly.

This type of fear was the last thing I expected of myself, especially since I was still an active-duty member. Somebody still must have had faith in me and the fact that I might recover at some point in the future. Honestly, I could not understand why I was trying to be so macho with the staff who were there to help me grow beyond my fears. I was probably on the verge of being confronted, and that is precisely what happened. The psychiatric nurse, a captain, laid it on the line very carefully, and for some reason, I was about to have a tough time accepting what he had to say. He was forthright, and he said I should avoid anything that had trauma, including the military. My life was going to change one way or another because the thought of leaving the military left me heartbroken to the point of a breakdown within itself.

My life was in the military throughout college and for three years after. No one had predicted war--it just happened, and I was left to execute proper judgment with the start of the war. At this point, I thought I would be paranoid to follow the captain's orders. The things he was preaching to me were true, and I had to measure my spirit and somehow comply. The captain was not done with his lecture yet. The most important thing about winning the fight with

PTSD was not to self-medicate with alcohol or drugs. That could be life-ending in itself. This seemed like an easy enough task, but I knew it would be stretching my resilience to the limit. I had to really think positively at this point to maintain an honest viewpoint, even with all the negatives, and I was determined to drive myself there, no matter what I had to endure.

This whole thing about having PTSD was starting to get really intense, and I began to wonder if I had the true energy to weather the psychiatric storm. I was a leader of men, and to talk about my negative feelings associated with PTSD was a weakness and against my better judgment, even if it was with a loved one. The captain assured me that breaking down the barriers would shatter the walls of isolation that kept me from being part of the real world. He recommended that I start seeing a talk therapist and taking medication to deal with anxiety and depression. The captain advised me that the therapy could be done individually or in groups. I was on such a sojourn, and at this point, I did not know which path to take. I just knew I had to change my attitude to adopt a new outlook. I wanted to progress and reach deep within myself to achieve my newfound potential. Rock Steady, Ever Ready, is an age-old motto that I hope will carry me to a new level of survival.

I stared up at the wall. The lecture I had just gotten from the psychiatric nurse/Captain had left my mind on fire, wondering if I truly had the capability of living up to my potential anymore. Living in the past was the easy thing to do at this point. I wanted to put on my uniform again and resume my position at the head of the formation. I knew it was a reality that I would never experience again as I tried to gain a little sleep with whatever was left of the twilight hours. I assumed I would never know what had become of my section in Iraq. I just hoped that they were able to take advantage of the same level of medical treatment that I was, even though I seemed somewhat of a failure in making progress with it.

At this point, my memory was nothing more than a blur. I don't recall the name of anyone on my medical treatment team, but I really didn't care. I should have been more honest and open with my medical team because without them, my life would have been nothing. At the moment, I looked out the window beside my hospital bed, hoping to catch a glimpse of the heavens, searching for an answer throughout the evening, starved for the answer my heart desired, trying to avoid the desperation that plagued my soul. I never thought that I was a God-fearing man until I had to deal with the pain and negativity that I had to now. My life needed fixing. Slowly, I drifted into a gentler slumber, hoping that my life would not have to deal with the unknown fears again.

Double Duty 1

It really scared me. The thoughts of a mental illness ruling my life. Little did I know what I was getting myself into. PTSD, depression, and bipolar disorder. Unfortunately, I had not been an outstanding student in college, so I knew little about any of them. There was no end to the insanity. It was a double awareness that scared me to no end. I felt like I was a slave to something I had no control over, except to come out fighting like a champ, except in this case, I didn't even know how to do that. I said no, I will not let this happen to me, but it took me two decades to realize that I had the potential to live up to that statement. This gave me the energy to say no, drive forward, and try to escape. I pleaded with my psychiatrist not to allow me to become a statistic as well.

Some 15 million people in America suffer from depression on an annual basis. Another 10 million suffer from bipolar illness. These are rather excellent numbers that can no longer be ignored. Depression sinks its roots in many forms, from major depression to seasonal affective disorder. Depression has no boundaries. It is an illness that not only affects people in the U.S., but worldwide as well. It interferes with concentration, motivation, and many other aspects of daily functioning. Reality dictates the complexity of depression that affects many aspects of the body. It may disrupt sleep and appetite, and in extreme cases, it can disturb weight gain or loss.

Along with the issues of having depression, medical professionals are plagued with the best way to deal with problems surrounding bipolar illness as well. Mood swings do not just reflect the good days and bad days that many people have, but being bipolar can introduce both manic and depressive issues that have an adverse negative effect, ranging from being supercharged with a tremendous euphoria to being extremely sad.

These high and low periods may happen separately, or there may be periods with elements of both. There is no time limit on how long a bipolar episode may last. Bipolar illness can create issues at work or in a social setting as well. It is hard to develop close personal relationships at work or in a personal setting. Many bipolar individuals have been plagued for years with how to best deal with these issues.

Pure madness was driving me at that point. My goal was to be an inspiration for people who suffer from manic-depressive issues, but I might have failed them and myself. To be plagued by either bipolar illness or depression borders on insanity. On many occasions, I wondered, "Why me?" but there was no answer. A mental illness creates a new dimension within that nobody deserves to have. You must have a hidden fortress within you to find the courage to correct your behavior and the strength to move forward.

Despite my trials and tribulations, I give full credit to those who have braved the storm before it was my turn. True inspiration had to come from somewhere. The things that kept driving me were knowing that I could succeed and that I was not in this fight alone. Then I questioned society as a whole: Why must I suffer? The statistics are against me, but I continue to fight. I have only faced death once, and I cheated it, but my insight tells me that one day my luck will run out and my fight to live will finally be cheated. Apparently, I have a hidden energy within myself that keeps me driving forward with a hunger for success. My role model discovered that he had bipolar disorder before me, but unfortunately, it went unchecked, and it ended up afflicting him at a later point in life. I give full credit for my success to the veterans and civilians who have been able to master the illness with the help of the appropriate medical authority. Their stories and convictions are like a personal fortress to me, with the hidden strength I so desire to add to my own arsenal.

In one out of ten people, a traumatic event will cause a cascade of psychological and biological changes known as post-traumatic stress disorder. Wars throughout the ages often triggered what was commonly known as shell shock. Returning soldiers from wartime environments were unable to adapt to civilian life. Although each successive war brings attention to this issue, it was not until the Vietnam War that the term PTSD was actually coined and became recognized by the psychiatric community as a grave mental illness that would create difficulty for veterans trying to adapt to a peacetime environment after being in the war. Now the goals of the mental health community are to help veterans and others adapt to PTSD and become successful in a regular environment. Ideal programs are seen in many VAs across the country, as veterans are revitalized once again to become part of reality.

The war was over. A psychiatric imbalance dashed my dreams of promotion. Now there was nothing but dreams, therapy, and trigger points. I found it hard to believe that imbalances and medication were ruling my life. I had reached so many points where I just didn't care, but medication and therapy had helped me restore the imbalance. So many times, I asked, "Why me?" but the issue would not be addressed for years. I have come to realize that some people develop post-traumatic stress disorder after living through any type of shock, such as a car wreck, sexual issues, or even giving birth to a child. I never really recognized the extent of trauma that a wide variety of problems can cause. As the old saying goes, I was only a lieutenant.

PTSD is when your body turns on a “fight or flight” response. In the face of something life-threatening, it revs up your heart rate, gets your muscles ready to run, and amps up stress hormones to fight off potential threats. Your brain tells its body that some of its functions are less important. The incredible level of hype turns off parts of the brain related to memory, emotion, and thinking. Normalcy has no meaning at this point as everything becomes undefined.

Even though I had a working definition of what a trigger point was, I was very reluctant to explore the issue because I had suffered on more than one occasion when I had been under too much pressure. PTSD still really frightened me because who knew when and where it would be set off. In my case, I had horrific experiences as both a soldier and a civilian that had caused more fright than what I knew how to deal with. I couldn’t recall how many sleepless nights I had had trying to escape the negativity associated with PTSD. I had loved the military, but I had suffered, then I had suffered some more, and the long part of the story was that I knew more pain was on its way. Being assigned to a Stryker brigade as the adjutant in Germany only spelled trouble because the mission of the Stryker brigade was to generate body count.

Before the war began, I was assigned as the community adjutant to the NATO/SHAPE Support Group in Mons, Belgium, but the geopolitical spectrum was changing quickly. It was inevitable that conflict loomed on the horizon, as a coalition of Middle Eastern countries faced the military might of rebel forces across the district. I never truly understood why military training was so intense until I got personal orders from the next higher headquarters to cross-level to Germany to the 5th Stryker Brigade. I had never been to a Stryker Brigade before, but I quickly realized that my first task was to learn wartime casualty reporting, which was part of the brigade adjutant's mission. I was young and foolish, so I said, "What the hell?" I had never been to war before, so this was something that might be a completely new experience, except for the trauma that I might be dealing with later after the initial deployment to Iraq.

There were going to be two orders of operations that I would definitely recall as my career melted away. I had been with the brigade for only four days when the first operations order took effect. Prepare for a five-mile run, brigade formation at 0500 the following morning. I couldn't imagine moving a unit the size of the 5th in an organized fashion for a five-mile run. Only time would tell if this task could be accomplished. I knew I was not going to sleep well that evening because, the following morning, maintaining the integrity of the brigade as the adjutant would be a huge accomplishment.

It was 0450 the following morning as the brigade started to form up. I heard the cadence being called by an unknown 1st Sergeant in Bravo Battalion, which sent a chill down my spine. I could listen to the echoes of the troop's cadence drift into the morning air. Bravo Battalion was ready for war.

The cadence went as follows:

> Walking through the desert.
>
> Kicking up the sand.
>
> That is when you know you are in Iran.
>
> You hear the choppers coming.
>
> They are coming overhead.

They are coming for the wounded and the dead.

> You jump into a foxhole.
>
> You find your buddy dead.
>
> He died from a bullet.

A bullet in his head.

I had never tasted the stress of combat before, but this cadence forged a new reality into my train of thought. I didn't want to foresee the moment when the Stryker Brigade was forced to see combat, because many of its members were young and foolish, not mature enough to resolve their own differences, including me. This is a reality that I really didn't want to embrace, but I had to openly admit I had personal struggles on more than one occasion. There was a function on my computer called body count, and I didn't want to use it and submit a negative report to the brigade commander. The commander had never fulfilled a combat mission, and I did want to be responsible for a new mission with the help of the chaplain when we went back stateside. Perhaps I might be labeled a coward at this point for seeing the negativity of my duties, but it was a reality that I didn't want to follow through on. If it came to that point where I had to endure the shock of meeting with loved ones or losing a new friend, I was not sure if I was equipped. I knew the moment of truth would soon be upon the brigade as we began our final approach to a combat environment. I hated to think of it that way, but the brigade was making its final preparations to move to its final Staima sight to draw equipment, but the question was where. Five thousand of us began cur five-mile run to prepare for the final operations order.

I recall my time with the NATO/SHAPE Support Group, where I was the adjutant. I thought that my taskings from the command division were easy enough to handle, but how quickly I forget that I was only a lieutenant, and, in all reality, nothing was expected of me. The commander sheltered and slowly mentored me, preparing me to become a brigade adjutant, where I would likely be put into a combat situation if the need ever arose. I was shaking at this point as the brigade finished its run, because the time had come. I just wondered if I was soldier enough to fulfill my mission. I was not a pretty first lieutenant at that point, and I knew little about the stressors that a soldier could experience before, during, and after a deployment. I had to exercise my duties and let fate take its course. Crossing that hurdle was going to be a rather tricky task, especially with the onset of manic-depressive behavior (more commonly known as bipolar) that I knew absolutely nothing about. I had been in Europe for almost two years, and I had not had an "episode" yet, but I could not label it even if someone asked me to.

I knew that the 5th Stryker Brigade was equipped to do its mission. The professionalism of all ranks was seen during the run, but my mind was not at peace for what loomed ahead. Combat battalions of men and women ran harmoniously over the five-mile trail. We were now ready for war. I had a new respect for the professionalism of the enlisted leader. Being enlisted did not give a soldier the edge--it just meant that you would die first. I spent two weeks with the command sergeant major, learning as much as possible about the brigade after completing my in-processing into the local military community. My fears persisted at that point, wondering if the dawn of tomorrow would bring me the peace of mind I desired. Only my energy in the morning twilight would allow me to determine that. My memory dims of what transpired when I was such a young soldier. If I had known that my mental health was in jeopardy, this would have been a journey that I never would have undertaken.

Why did I always do this to myself? I would formulate a question that only I could answer. As I looked up into the starlight, I pondered my thoughts. I didn't know if it was amazement or fear that drove me to the edge on many a sleepless night. My mind wouldn't stop. The thoughts and ideas that I generated were incredible. I wondered whether anyone else, in general, had such issues with creative dynamics. For some reason, I didn't want to fear being creative because it made me stand out from the crowd. Little did I know that this insecurity about being creative would get me retired from the military. I was very uncomfortable with myself at this point, let alone tolerate the harshness from senior-ranking staff officers. With the mission over the horizon, I had to be firm, for my section depended on me to provide leadership to bring them home after the mission was completed. I was wondering if the dawn of tomorrow would bring me peace of mind, much less identify the mission of the 5th Stryker Brigade. Five thousand strong, we all waited through the twilight hours, praying that we would all come home. Little did I know that my stray thoughts would leave me devastated the following morning and move me forward in a direction I didn't expect.

Throughout the twilight, my thoughts began to spin. I couldn't help myself. Everything became so rapid and spontaneous that I began to fear. For what, I wasn't sure, but nothing made sense at this point. I knew I had responsibilities in the office, but I could not function properly. I needed help; I couldn't function properly to get it; I couldn't even recall the services provided by the local hospital. My thoughts screamed, and my brain cycled everything so quickly. Somehow, I managed to get to my phone to try to put an end to the drama. However, I didn't realize that these dramas were a new reality. Finally, after a complete fumble trying to find the station hospital's number, an ambulance was dispatched. The ambulance was the beginning of the end for my tenure of duty with the 5th Stryker Brigade. I had failed in my mission before it had even gotten off the ground. I didn't know it then, but I was on the verge of losing my job and my commission without a thorough line-of-duty investigation. At this point, I just wanted the pain to go away and be complete like everyone else. I screamed out in agony as the military paramedics raced into my apartment to try to relieve the pain. Little do I recall beyond that point. However, I was soon to find out, when I awoke, that my military career was over, and I would have some inkling of what was torturing me. I had never imagined that mental illness had entered my life, but I was naive enough to know what it was. Little did I know that my military saga was about to come to an end and that my life would be changed forever. My night was to be filled with the worst that any person could have.

I woke up early in the morning, expecting to take personal accountability. Instead, the brigade commander was by my bedside talking to the doctor before he spoke to me. My charging body was in restraints to keep me from moving unnecessarily because only the Lord knew if I was going to look beyond myself and try to take my life. The brigade commander had been like a father figure to me, and he was gentle in speech even though I could tell he was disappointed at what had begun to happen. Gently, he spoke, asking me how I felt. I tried to muster a grin, but I couldn't. The brigade commander got very tired and said, "Son, you need to let your medical professionals help you if you want a chance to survive and move forward." My thoughts were "I was not ready to give up", but I was very weak when I spoke. The Colonel recognized that I was trying to be macho, but he bowed his head and remarked that the real war for me was about to start. Little did I know that PTSD plagued me, and perhaps a touch of bipolar illness at that point. The brigade commander just leaned over me and said, "May God help you at this point." With those parting remarks, the commander consulted with the doctor, then began his journey back to the brigade, with orders to resume preparations for war. I didn't understand exactly what had transpired, but I was sure the events would unfold over time.

The journey was about to continue for my individual soul. I could not even recall what had put me into the station hospital, and I had not even been briefed by the doctor yet as to why I had not been admitted. Little did I know that the doctor who had admitted me was a psychiatrist. I tried to sit up in bed, but the grips around my arms restrained me. I couldn't imagine what had transpired throughout the evening to get me strapped down in bed. I hung my head in shame, for I began to realize what might have happened throughout the evening. I recall stress. I knew very little about psychiatric illnesses, but I knew what PTSD was, for I had met many veterans in my professional path who had experienced it. The psychiatrist finally came to my bedside. I just lay in silence while he talked to me, for this was something I needed to hear firsthand without interruption. My only thought at this point was centered on my military career. Was it over or not? The psychiatrist was slowly getting to that point. However, he alluded to the fact that I was suffering from PTSD that might lead to other things, such as bipolar illness. I didn't know what bipolar was at that point, but I guessed that it would end my career.

PTSD and Creativity

There is compelling evidence that suggests that creativity can be closely linked to trauma. Dr. Marie Forgeard conducted an online survey to investigate this thought. An online survey was created and administered to participants who were clinically noted to have endured a traumatic situation. The results were measured to compare trauma and creativity.

She found that "adversity-induced distress predicted self-reported creative growth and breadth in a sample of online participants. Cognitive processing (intrusive deliberative rumination) as well as domains of post-traumatic growth/depreciation--in particular, self-reported changes in interpersonal relationships and unforeseen perceptions of new possibilities for one's own life mediated the link between self-reported distress and creativity outcomes."

One of the most challenging issues for an individual with a mental health condition is tangential thinking. This may disrupt personal confidence, individual personal relationships, and other intangible issues. I have worked to avoid personal relationships because of the stressors involved. Sometimes the strength of a friendship is enough to help an individual through tough times. At this point, I think I am finding a way to face many faults within myself due to my battles with PTSD and bipolar illness. I am just finding a new way to combat these issues and move myself to a new level.

A strike from the Unknown

The sweat broke off my brow as I was helo'd out as a replacement to the 3rd/73rd Infantry. After seven years as a grunt, I felt I had developed my skills to become a complete infantry soldier. My goal was to become a platoon sergeant, but I had to survive this mission first. I had the confidence to do the mission. However, I was faced with this mission first, and I hoped it would give me the necessary credibility to move to that level if I survived. Despite the stifling heat, I was not afraid to take on this mission and demonstrate leadership once more. I deserved the promotion to the next level win, lose, or draw on this mission.

Dust cleared as the helo settled down in the landing zone at the battalion's base camp. So, this was my new home, I thought. It was a far cry from Fort Benning, but I embraced the challenge. With orders in hand, I was immediately greeted by the platoon leader. I was amazed as the bird lifted off and headed back to the brigade headquarters, which it called home. Realizing I was in a combat zone in the middle of Kuwait, I instantly recognized that the platoon leader wanted my attention. He was a rather stocky fellow, built for the life of the infantry. This was a second home for him as well, and he lived and breathed his duty and commitment to the country.

The platoon leader motioned for me to follow him to the company commander's hutch, which I did without a moment's hesitation. As a trained soldier, I would not hesitate to follow my leadership through thick and thin. To my surprise, I was greeted at the hutch door by the First Sergeant. It was very unusual for a platoon leader, the First Sergeant, and the Company commander to all be on the same premises within a combat zone. Something was definitely in the air. Relying on the past seven years of developed infantry savvy, I realized that this was a meeting of great importance. The platoon leader quickly caught the company commander's eye. I could tell the commander was nervous and wanted to make this meeting short. Finally, the commander broke the hard silence and went into brief detail about the op plan for the upcoming mission, in which, unknown to me, I would play a crucial role.

Without hesitation, the commander spoke of the patrol the platoon would be engaged in, and, to my chagrin, he told me I would be walking point.

This is not exactly what I wanted to hear, especially since this was my first combat tour in seven years, and I was already in jeopardy. I did not want to be a platoon sergeant that quickly, but orders were orders. There was no intelligence posted in the briefing that said I would be endangering myself unnecessarily. With that, the commander dismissed the platoon leader and me to begin preparation for the patrol. Saying that, the platoon leader escorted me to the part of the compound where the platoon's bivouac site was. I was going to share a hutch with two other platoon members, Bones and Jeffrey. Their true character would be seen throughout the twilight as the platoon prepared for the patrol.

Bones was a unique character who was studying medicine online in the middle of Kuwait. He was also the platoon's corpsman. Jeffrey was a squad leader. He probably saw me as being relatively naive for agreeing to walk point on my first assignment. Bones kind of followed suit with Jeffrey, but informed me he would work really hard to relieve me of any injuries I might incur while walking point. I was ready to protest this type of euphoric welcoming, but I guess time would tell how good their insights were. As the dusk settled over the horizon, I cleaned my weapon one last time before preparing for the platoon muster. This was the last time I would see the company base camp. As the platoon fell into formation, we proceeded to the ammunition to draw 9 clips of 5.56 ammunition. At this point, I felt completely ready to kick some Arabic tail.

Waiting for the order to lock and load one twenty-round clip of ammunition, I was ready to light up some Arabic ass if it would only be that easy! Bones saw I was on edge and casually came over to calm my nerves, saying, "I got you covered." Not what I wanted to hear from the Corpsman, but in a way, it was reassuring. The platoon leader also made his presence felt, brusquely asking me if I understood the op order issued by the company commander. Nobody had briefed me on the strength of the unfriendly forces in the area, and given that I was walking point, it left me a little concerned, but it would not deter me from the mission. I had confidence and knew the rules of engagement. The platoon leader gave the signal to move. The company commander had briefed me well on the potential route of movement, and if there was any engagement during the patrol, I was not going to shirk my duties.

Every step was an endless grind that showed no mercy as I sank into sand up to my ankles. The late afternoon dragged on, and my vision became more and more strained as the twilight set in. I became edgy. I didn't know what to expect. Suddenly, I felt a trip wire go off, but it was too late. The flare went off, and I felt a bullet rip into my body, forcing me into a state of painful unconsciousness. I remember nothing from that point forward no Bones and no call for Medevac.

Before the Gulf conflict, the term PTSD meant nothing to me, even while I attended all the military training I needed for deployment. No one complained about mental illnesses, much less PTSD. As I sat there in my hospital bed, somewhat stricken by the entire course of events, reading my hospital records, I became more aware of the issues surrounding PTSD. It made me feel like I had a deficit that I would never be able to overcome. I was determined to become whole again, but I was faced with a whole new reality. It was like a bad dream that hindered my every waking moment. The only thing I could do was ask myself, "Why me?" The trauma invaded my senses (or what I perceived to be my senses) and was causing my life to move forward in a warped fashion.

My confidence in my abilities as a soldier had been rocked. I had lost track of all the time since I had been medivacked from the desert. Peace of mind was unreachable, and my thoughts left me on edge in a daily struggle of self-betrayal. The only thing that I really understood about PTSD was that I was suffering greatly, and I was thoroughly incapable of self-analyzing a solution to resolve the agony. I frequently relived the experience of that dreadful night out in the desert. My mind could not get beyond the clumsiness of the moment when I walked into the sniper's bullet.

My mind was possessed by an insanity and panic that I couldn't comprehend. My thoughts flashed as if I were reliving the pain of the moment where the sniper's bullet had entered my chest. My breathing labored intensely. I envisioned the pain that existed only in my mind. It seemed to be a cruel dream that I had lived in reality. My mind reached out for that unforeseen reality that was beyond the stressors of yesteryear. I was scorned, burnt, lost in the moment, and devastated. I wondered if I could grasp the true essence of what I was experiencing. The only thing that was continually made evident was that I was a wounded veteran with a mental illness. I was angry not only with myself but also for not having the courage to step up and face the harshness I had to deal with.

The years have gone by, and I have grown as an individual once again, except that a mental disability somewhat plagues me. I have improved my life from the early years, but I still suffer some effects of PTSD. In addition to my own battles, I have seen the impact of PTSD in others as well. It is a far-reaching and devastating disorder. Its symptoms usually have an adverse effect that can destroy an individual's mental health, physical health, work life, and personal relationships. I was no exception.

Experts have discovered throughout the years that individuals with PTSD are at much greater risk for developing other mental health disorders, such as anxiety disorders, depression, eating disorders, substance abuse, and suicidal ideation. I could only dream of the day when my trauma would finally end, and when my issues dealing with PTSD would become a thing of the past. I didn't know if this was possible, but I was willing to take the chance. I searched high and low inside my feelings, looking for the key to self-satisfaction, not knowing in which direction to turn. I was constantly confused as to what would be the guiding light. Then an unforeseen force reached out and touched me, urging me to relax. The answer starts here.

Reading actually gave me a new lease on life. I knew beyond a shadow of a doubt that I was doomed to be plagued by PTSD for the rest of my life, but what I was not prepared for was how devastating it was. I was never a big fan of military health journals, but for once, I was determined to pay attention. The study I was ordered to peruse by a nurse was a very recent publication by the Center for Military Health. Research indicated that out of 1.64 million service members who were deployed to the Middle East, approximately 300,000 troops returned with either PTSD or traumatic brain injury (TBI). I could not imagine what TBI was like, because my energies had been solely focused on PTSD.

My curiosity was piqued just by reading further into the health study. I had a craving for the obvious at this point, except that I was kind of naive about the whole issue. I went on to learn the basics of PTSD. PTSD can be linked to any reaction associated with trauma, and TBI can be related to any type of impact or trauma associated with the brain. Unfortunately, despite the carnage caused by these types of injuries, nothing is apparent because they are invisible to others. This was an experience that had not yet been linked to my personal life. I was a man possessed, on a mission to find the source of my imperfection. I kept on reading about two methods of treatment that had been useful in treating PTSD: psychotherapy and medication.

Professional therapy or counseling can help you understand your thoughts and reactions, and learn techniques to deal with challenging situations. Research has shown that there are specific types of counseling that are more effective for treating PTSD than others. Medication can also be used in the battle with PTSD. Medication can help people living with PTSD deal with tension and adjustment issues, as well as potentially improve sleep. It really took a lot of self-examination, but I felt I could win this challenge and become a complete person again if I applied myself in the treatment phase.

Author's Note:

Since 1980, PTSD referred to as the "inability of a person to process trauma that may have resulted from exposure to war, physical or sexual violence, terrorism, or natural disasters" (Bauer, 2015). Clinicians are aware of how PTSD affects the patient, the spouse or partner, children, other family members, friends, the outside community in general, and the mental health community as a whole. There can be moral injury as a result of being exposed to PTSD. Trauma can affect how individuals interpret their spiritual, moral, or ethical understanding of the importance of being accepted within the human race and of having a personal relationship with God. In the foreseeable future, PTSD will continue to exist as a challenge as our story of trauma unfolds from the carnage of Afghanistan, Iraq, Operation Desert Shield, Desert Storm, Vietnam, Korea, and even the residual effects of World War II.

The therapist made me feel that my treatment was finally being handled in a teamwork environment, and my thoughts were more accurate about PTSD and less distressing. This also laid the groundwork for me to better cope with anger, guilt, and fear. I quit blaming myself for the traumatic events that were beyond my power to change. The cognitive therapy helped me understand that the trauma that happened to me was not my fault. Perhaps it was time to learn to forgive myself for what happened in the past. I had tortured my inner self for all those years, and I never really understood why.

For years, I had continued to say that the mishap in Iraq was entirely my fault because I was not more alert. Still, my therapist made me realize that most accidents in combat happen beyond the control of any level of leadership. To openly admit that this was not my fault and that I was being too hard on myself was something I might come to terms with over time. I was battling a personal evil, and only time would tell whether I would truly be the complete victor in this battle for my soul.

Author's Note:

There are also several other types of therapy besides CBT. Exposure therapy is based on the idea that people learn to fear thoughts and feelings based on the fact that they remind them of a past traumatic event. By talking about your fears repetitively with a therapist, you will learn to gain control of your thoughts and the negativity of the trauma. Without question, you will know there is no reason to fear your trauma.

Therapy also helps you control stress and think positively once again. With the guidance of your therapist, you can learn to change how you feel about stressful events over time. Therapy helps you learn to focus on positive memories before taking on the challenges posed by negative thoughts that may be preventing you from progressing. This is called "desensitization," and it helps you deal with the worst memories a little at a time. Your therapist may ask you to deal with the worst memories a little bit at a time. This will help you desensitize yourself to what it may feel like to be overwhelmed in some capacity. There are many other types of emotional therapy for managing thoughts and situations related to trauma. Breathing and relaxation techniques can help calm an individual when side effects of "triggers" occur. These coping mechanisms create a means of improvement in positively redefining the individual. This can also improve coping skills. This can allow the individual to help accept their lot in life, and it can provide the individual with much-needed PTSD psycho-education.

Being in a combat environment will really stress an individual out. Beyond a shadow of a doubt, many individuals had braved many significant and life-changing events, but combat was an unknown of its own. Many individuals didn't know it then, but they have since come to realize how combat would affect the rest of their lives, especially for those who were close. It was just hard to realize how important it was to get help to manage the upside of recovery effectively. Many people in recovery are loners, but getting loved ones involved is absolutely crucial. Turning to old friends in the military seemed like a good idea as I tried to find cohorts in arms who might have understood me as a youth and could reach out to me on current issues.

I just wanted to know the truth, but I couldn't explain why I was always on edge. The nightmares that I dreaded and couldn't avoid were endless from one night to the next. Even with Dr. Hall's assistance, it was a hopeless struggle. The terror had to stop. My resolution to this whole complexity was to spend more and more time at home, locked away from reality. I was determined to find some resolution for this, to find some peace of mind so that my family and I could have peace and tranquility together. Once again, I started therapy at the local Veterans' Administration to try to overcome my difficulties. I heard about how good revised treatments were at the VA, but after so many years of a losing battle, I wondered if I should fight for myself to try again.

To my surprise, I was matched with a therapist who was a master of cognitive-behavioral therapy. My attention was finally piqued. Research shows that CBT is the most commonly utilized therapy for veterans with PTSD. In cognitive therapy, your therapist helps you understand and change how you think about your trauma and its negative aftermath. Your goal is to know how specific thoughts affect your trauma, cause stress, and make your symptoms worse. My goal, even though I didn't recognize it if I had any goals then, was to learn more about the stresses and illnesses caused by PTSD, which my therapist reinforced.

The Beginning of Completeness

Ole John looked me straight in the eye when he saw the title of my new book. He just stared at it for a moment, and I thought for some reason or another that the title was not to his liking. However, he came out and clearly stated that it was everything he had expected. That was my cue to be silent and listen to his critique, because the great lawyer was about to lecture me on the hard-earned facts of life. The trail I had been down paled in comparison to what the warrior had been through. To this day, I have never figured out whether calling him "ole" was appropriate, even though I have known John for what seems like a millennium. John knew about the horrors of PTSD firsthand, which I had never really experienced at all. In reality, a candy striper had more experience with PTSD than I did.

John, on the other hand, knew firsthand about the mental difficulties of PTSD. John had survived warfare, whereas I had only interviewed gentlemen like him to uncover a hidden truth the world wanted to know. I hesitated to approach him about the mental anguish he had suffered during the Vietnam conflict. Vietnam was a war of attrition, in which Ole John was clearly a survivor. I could only appreciate the infinite teachings that John would give me on the topic because, in reality, I was clueless when it came to the undying mental pains of enduring PTSD.

Ole John often relived the horrors of his Vietnam military service, and he was not afraid to communicate those issues to me. He dealt with PTSD symptoms on and off and their impact on his daily life, but nothing seemed evident in his ongoing struggle then. Despite these trials, Ole John remained firmly in control and contributed significantly to the wealth of information that shaped our conversation.

His brusqueness had me silenced. I wasn't sure what would happen next, which bothered me. So, acting instinctively, I got up and got both of us a cup of coffee. We sat in silence, giving the wise man a chance to collect his thoughts. Even though I had to push on with our interview, I knew when to provide the retired Sergeant First Class some breathing room. Finally, with a gentle nod, he gave me his approval to start up the conversation once again. I knew when the big fellow wanted to talk and didn't want to talk. I usually guided interviews with wartime veterans, but Ole John, being a man of leadership and character, assumed a different path. His focus was on his mission, so I let him speak his mind without interruption.

Ole John was well-versed on various topics that affected his military career. Still, he was never open about why he had joined the Army or the commitment and intensity that he had made to the military during his Basic Training years. To make a long story short, he joined in 1968 when he was naïve and unsure if he was ready to handle the unforeseen realities of life. Vietnam was all over the news, and he thought he could make an impact with his patriotic fervor. Another primary reason Ole John enlisted in the military was that he believed he could become a better person. Ole John had done exceptionally well on the Armed Forces tests, qualifying for many jobs that required intellectual insight. However, despite his overpowering intelligence, he elected to attend the infantry training course at Ft. Dix, New Jersey, where most recruits from the Northeast went.

At the onset of the Vietnam conflict, Ft. Dix looked very much as it had during World War II. The barracks had not changed, and the reception station was much the same. Within a few days, his in-processing was completed, and Ole John looked like the true American soldier, government-issue all the way. Welcome to Basic Training.

It was high-speed Basic Training, in fact. The drill instructor "broke" individual soldiers into solitary fighting machines, then remolded them into a fighting team prepared for the jungles of

Southeast Asia. With successful psychology and training, the personal ego was stripped down to nothing. At this point in his narrative, Ole John looked at me and quietly said, "If I wasn't a man when I started basic training, I was when I graduated and marched down Doughboy Field on the last day of training."

The drill sergeant was the person in the military to be feared. "He was our mama and papa for almost nine weeks. He said, "Move," and, as a unit, we asked how fast. He had us cleaning the barracks every night, plus pulling fireguard." Ole John muttered under his breath at this point and simultaneously chuckled. This was one experience he did not outgrow quickly until his wife told him so years later. Somehow, at that point, he knew he had outgrown his drill instructor. Unfortunately, by then, he still had the harsh reality of Vietnam in his psyche.

After Ole John returned home, he became a college graduate. He made good use of his personal time after Vietnam. He had a true intellectual spirit. He was patriotic and wanted to give where he could provide without getting emotionally broken in the process. He never explained why, but he had many apprehensions about reporting for active duty, yet was determined to look beyond that, complete his tour, and continue serving his country in some form. He wanted to make the best of his situation because it seemed the right thing to do, and military service gave him the character to keep charging forward and realize that others needed his strengths. Unfortunately, his tour in Vietnam had left him terrified of life itself.

It befuddled me, but I could see the terror in Ole John's eyes. I was merely a writer, yet I could imagine the chaos and pain that invaded Ole John's thoughts while he was in the steamy jungles of Vietnam. Was it possible that I didn't or couldn't understand the internal conflicts and issues that Ole John had to deal with then and now? He classified himself at that point in life as being a grunt, which is something I didn't understand.

In my own military life, I was classified solely as combat service support. I was part of the office team running personnel issues for a completely different part of the theater. My chosen life path at this point was to be a writer and help others understand the day-to-day issues that plagued our fallen heroes. I could not relate to the agony and stress Old Joe had to endure daily.

Ole John was a unique breed of man. True, he got drafted, but that meant nothing, especially with the war going at the pace it was. I assumed that the gentle giant was of the Camelot generation and willing to conduct himself like a gentleman of that era. He was fulfilling his patriotic duty by going to Vietnam, even if he was only a grunt. He had no regrets in his life about the decision he had made, even though, apparently, he later suffered heavily from PTSD.

Ole John waded ashore in South Vietnam in the first half of 1968, convinced he was the champion of a cause. No matter how extreme the situation he was in, he thought he was destined for success and that he would triumph over the evil forces of Communism. He had no fear of the Viet Cong or the North Vietnamese. His internal belief was that his unit would prevail by the time his first tour was complete. Unfortunately, these were very idealistic beliefs that he had no fear of sharing with anyone. To him, Communism was wrong, and he was the champion of democracy.

While he was not afraid of being idealistic, he wondered how he would react to the physical and psychological fatigue associated with the trauma of war. When he finally left South Vietnam, even his most idealistic convictions about his mission were shaken. The beliefs and ideals he held about his country were no longer as steadfast as they once were. I was stunned by the way Ole John referenced his belief in democracy. His thoughts then were incomplete and ruptured. He even seemed estranged and at a loss for words when he talked. He was shaken in his belief in duty, honor, and country, as well as in whether his country did the right thing by his standards. I couldn't give Ole John a straight answer on that matter, because I was from a different era and my thoughts were different than his. My stressors and emotional differences were more ideological and from a different time.

It was quite an experience for Ole John when he was in South Vietnam. He was probably shocked when his company was not greeted by hostile fire. Young soldiers were not automatically gunned down and left to wither in pools of their own blood by the Viet Cong. He was frightened by what was expected of him and culture-shocked by his first foreign country. He knew it would take time to adjust to his new surroundings; however, normalcy seemed impossible in a combat zone.

At first, Ole John would not share his personal life with me because of his time in combat. I encouraged him to reach outside of his comfort zone, prying him to enter the memories of the negative hell that he had gone through. It was almost suffocating for him to relive the intense heat and humidity that made life completely unbearable for him in Vietnam. The foul smells of rotting flesh, garbage, and decaying plant life, along with the almost intolerable body sweat, intensified the silent agony of the remote individual hell that each soldier experienced. Ole John was like an island facing a storm, drawing on his inner strength to survive. I couldn't even imagine the inner torture that this silent hero was putting himself through, knowing that he would never allow himself to quit.

Ole John began to waver under my questioning. He began to drift off, reflecting on his trials and tribulations, complaining about the conditions he endured, which made it difficult for him to accept the future. He was his own island, trying to cope with this interview, in which it seemed like I was endlessly grilling him on the strengths and weaknesses that had come back to haunt him at every step of his tour in Vietnam. I stared into Ole John's eyes, looking deep into his soul. I could see that he was deeply angered. He had been committed to a lockdown ward at a VA hospital for fighting for his country. This was an action he didn't understand.

PTSD was a new issue for him, and he was struggling to deal with it. Like many a volunteer or draftee, he thought he was fighting as a hero, and he was never afraid to risk his own life to save a fellow soldier's. Overcoming fear allowed him to fulfill what he believed was his destiny, potentially, but he was never absolutely confident it was.

The most challenging personal mission that Ole John faced was coming back to the States to unite himself with his old girlfriend -- a love that was not meant to be. He was more afraid of rejection from her at that point than from taking a bullet from the Viet Cong. The emotional duress left him scarred, if not downright scared. His fear of reality led him to re-enlist for another tour, which was probably a mistake, but it left him more upset than before. The only thing he was ready to do at this point was damn his own soul.

Being a grunt exposed Ole John to the deadliest warfare the world had to offer, which was conducted by booby traps and snipers. The killing process was accomplished by death and dismemberment. The Viet Cong and North Vietnamese had many advantages when it came to doing this, which included knowledge of the area and often the cooperation of the civilians. The enemy excelled, becoming a creative killing machine. When it came to demonstrating their field craft, they applied silent movement, noise discipline, and camouflage. When our side counterattacked, their advantages were courage, better weaponry, and deadly marksmanship.

Ole John began to stare off into the horizon at this point. I felt I should ask forgiveness for what I had done to my friend, but somehow, he was beginning to settle into his life. One thing that haunts a vet is the unnecessary loss of life. Ole John would not address this issue, but I could see he was frustrated and angry. It seemed like death was a constant companion in his life, in which there would always be an actual loss of innocence and companionship.

An Endless Struggle

It was a mental struggle I couldn't win. The nightmares were endless, repeating one night after another. Sudden noises made me jump out of my skin. Most of my time was spent isolated at home. I wondered if the trauma would ever stop. Was this my new world: PTSD, shell shock, or combat stress?

I felt like I was losing control over my life. I had witnessed people being harmed, and the shock was more than I could bear. The platoon leader bragged about saving countless American lives, but what about the numerous lives we took in the process without any regard? Perhaps he had a point, but a kid we killed had been only about twelve. For me, it was not a fair assessment to make, even though I was dealing with issues caused by the enemy's desire to hurt me in place of them.

The first time I came down with PTSD, I couldn't define what it was. I didn't take the time in the early 90s to research it, probably because I was foolish. I also didn't listen to the subtle hints, explanations, or thoughts of my medical treatment team. Over time, I learned my lessons in life about PTSD. As my knowledge base grew, I knew that some of the most common symptoms of PTSD included recurring memories or nightmares, sleepless nights, loss of interest or feeling numb, unexplainable anger, and being brash and irritable. In most cases, these symptoms do not emerge unless the vet is engaged in a conflict.

This unfortunate occurrence can cause a daily struggle in the civilian lives of many veterans. Veterans need to realize that even if they have PTSD, it doesn't mean they have to live with it. Hundreds of thousands of veterans have gotten treatment for PTSD and combat stress. Believe it or not, the treatment works. I received treatment for PTSD at the VA. I thought it was successful, but being the young and arrogant lieutenant I was, I thought I had mastered it without question silly me. However, a member of my medical treatment team was quite frank with me and pulled me aside, kindly advising me that I might want to rethink my thoughts on PTSD. Oh, she was so completely correct.

At that point in the rehabilitation process, two types of treatment were known for treating the illness: counseling and medication, which can help keep you focused on understanding your thoughts and secrets and discovering ways to cope with your feelings. Certain medications help you feel less worried and sad.

There can be a wide range of symptoms that indicate you are experiencing signs of PTSD. You can feel upset when things remind you of what happened that caused the emotional disaster. Nightmares can be never-ending and incredibly vivid, which can lead to flashbacks of the event that make you feel that everything is about to come crashing down all over again.

I am not always entirely sure of myself, but I am sure that more than one veteran has been left feeling emotionally drained, cut off from others, or living on the edge of fear itself. On many occasions, veterans have felt numb and empty, losing interest in things that their heart and soul once enjoyed. This leaves them emotionally drained and on the verge of becoming depressed, perhaps thinking they are always in personal danger, wondering why they constantly feel anxious and lost, jittery and irrational. Sometimes I wondered why I experienced panic attacks myself. I couldn't recollect what had happened in the past and the difficulty it had caused me.

On the way to Combat

This is a story that only the troop leader could tell. Combat is an issue many have struggled with for a long time. I don't know exactly where to begin when it came to the atrocities of Belgium that took me to the military community in Pirmasens, only to put me on a shortcut to Iraq, where I dealt with my first really traumatic event. My ignorance of being a lieutenant was about to show as I led my first relief section to one of our sister personnel service companies that was on the outer fringes of Baghdad. I had been in the country for only a matter of hours, serving as the officer in charge of our two small five-ton trucks being sent to the 207th PSC, which had been attached to the 21st Personnel Group for short-term personnel support. The voyage to the 207th seemed to be routine. Within seconds, I learned about the treacheries of convoy duty and experienced pure trauma.

I saw the trip wire going across the road only seconds too late when the front side of the five-ton was blown off. Within milliseconds, the driver of the vehicle had his head crashed into the steering column of the truck, and I was tossed out of my seat through the windshield of the five-ton. I felt blood streaming down my face, but I was too stunned to notice it. I was concerned about my section in the back end of my truck, but I was too dazed to do anything about it. I had become a true casualty of war.

Confused and afraid, I began to stir in my sleep, not understanding what had just transpired. Any noise frightened me. I struggled to recall what had happened. I looked around, waiting for someone to tell me. I tried to get out of bed, but leather straps bound me in. It was not a time to test my muscular development. My vision was hazy, and it was as if I couldn't get anyone's attention to tell me what had happened. I wanted to reach out and touch someone, to get them close to me and find out exactly where I was and what had happened to me. Finally, what appeared to be an orderly approached me, but only when I was in a completely exhausted state of mind did they say anything to me. I didn't know it at the time, but I was battling PTSD, which was something I could not overcome in my current state of mind. I was very distressed. I had lived through events that most people couldn't comprehend, but I couldn't even fathom what was unraveling in my mind. The anger was building up within me. I almost wanted to hate myself.

It angered my soul that I had dealt with this personal mental agony by myself. This was a hidden anger I couldn't share with anyone. The world didn't understand. Hell, I didn't even understand the secret horrors of PTSD, and I had been diagnosed with it. I just asked for someone to reach out and help me at that point. Every day brought a new level of mental anguish into my life. I floundered searching for the correct answers. I never had the right words to explain this to my medical team whenever one of them reached out to ask what I was feeling at that moment.

The old solution from the support team was to write down my fears. I always felt I was damning myself, but I didn't know any other way to express what I was experiencing then, and I wasn't willing to express my fears to the rest of the world, no matter what the reason. I knew I deserved the right for someone to help me understand the trauma that was plaguing me, but I didn't care who I had to ask or why I had to ask. I just vaguely remember the horrors of the event, and nothing more.

Why I let this plague me, I will never know. However, I did, and this was becoming a reality that would haunt me in the confines of my own lost world. Not a night went by that I wasn't feeling on edge. Nightmares pursued me to no end; the atrocities and the negativities of stress and illness haunted me. The violence made me jump when my nerves should have been at peace. Thirty years later, I shake my head at the physical and psychological damage I have suffered, and I witness other troops and the pain they have suffered as well.

I had only begun to grasp the fears that had beset my mind. I had experienced something that most people would never understand. I had been placed in danger, and this is how my mind was still reacting that night. Perhaps this was a feeling that meant nothing if I was that lucky. I wanted to read or do something to keep the stressors or troubles of the past from becoming a part of my sleep. However, I was afraid to let my guard down, even for a moment. A deep, restless energy kept me from closing my eyes. The clock approached midnight, and I still had not drifted off into silence, nor had I achieved peace of mind. I desperately wanted to enjoy a quiet evening.

Finally, I thought I was about to be in a gentle sleep. Then fear crossed my mind with the thought of blood by my bedside. Explosions ripped through the air as a tripwire went off into the night. I knew I had lived through this once, but it was happening again. I wanted to get up out of the sand, but my paralysis wouldn't let me. My section was counting on me, but I was in so much pain and agony that I couldn't respond to cries for help. I felt a gentle grasp on my shoulder, trying to shake the fear out of me. Her gentle voice confronted me, urged me to wake up. "Sir, it was a trigger in your sleep," she said. I knew what the term *helpless* was at that point. I had to outgrow this somehow, someway.

Even though I thought I was safe in a psychiatric ward at Walter Reed Hospital, I was still petrified by reality. What had happened in Iraq seemed like yesterday, and my moments of failure seemed like they had just occurred minutes ago. My brain sensed danger, but my body reacted before I had time to think. I became angry and afraid, just responding to adrenaline and anxiety. I don't know what made me react the way I did, but it happened quickly and was extreme. I don't even know what "triggered the memories." What I thought would be an incredible night of sleep had turned into complete horror. I begged myself for an evening of peace and tranquility, but with the outbursts and hostile behavior, it was not meant to work out that way. I didn't want to express negativity to anyone, but I was afraid that other patients or staff would be frightened of my outbursts. What I had hoped would go right in my life was not happening, and I was bewildered. Would anything ever turn out right?

The big question for me was "What was the treatment plan for the PTSD?" Things weren't going well for me, and I needed someone to share some positive insights to brighten my day. It was as if the nurse had read my mind as she brought in my breakfast. I had not slept at all, and I was silently angry about what had happened the previous night. My life seemed to be in a downward spiral right then, and I was open to and would appreciate anything that would have brightened the day. The nurse talked to me in an incredibly polite fashion and calmly informed me that I would have my first workshop that morning on how to deal with PTSD. I looked at her quizzically. I had presumed by the way the previous night had gone that this was the way I was going to have to live my life. Slowly, a smile came across my face, for I realized the dejected mood I had had the previous night was not permanent.

Later, in the morning, one of the psychiatric nurses calmly walked into my room and told me he was there to brief me on the PTSD treatment. He was a commissioned officer from the Vietnam era, and that impressed me. We talked about the events of the previous night. The Captain clearly saw the dejection on my face and realized it was time for the experts at Walter Reed to take charge of my rehabilitation. I thought this was going to be a relatively unprofessional experience, but I could see that the decision was made to give me the best treatment. It was going to be an intense and incredible experience as I learned how to conquer all the fears from the previous night.

The Captain wasted no energy or time in talking about the "triggers" of the previous night. He was particular in his narration and said I should avoid people, places, and things that reminded me of the trauma. My triggers were psychological. The Captain gravely informed me that as his patient, he would address these issues at the briefing.

Life in the war zone is so much different than life at home. My daily routine was interrupted by something more stressful and chaotic than most people will ever experience. The events had driven me to the edge and beyond. My only reaction was to hide my feelings about the stress around me. Even though I was home safe in the hospital, I was haunted by nightmares and unwanted memories of what had transpired on the front. Memories of that explosion dominated every working memory I had. I was angry and blamed myself for not seeing the trip wire. I felt I had let ignorance replace my judgment. I blamed myself for not being aware of what happened to the rest of the team. Even though I was an officer, I could only damn my soul for not being more responsible.

At first, my psychiatrist merely observed me for nearly a month. I was so caught up in my own inner traumas that I really didn't pay attention to the complete reality of having PTSD or any semi-awkward feelings. Unexpectedly, we just started talking. Well, to be more honest about it, he did most of the talking, and I tried to make sense of why I was feeling more traumatized daily. He was quick to say in a somewhat oblivious fashion that I was experiencing symptoms of PTSD, but he couldn't explain why I was keeping the feelings bottled up and why I couldn't release the negativity. I believed that my thoughts on the issue were about to be corrected, and I was about to fear many unknown factors as to what the downside of PTSD actually was.

Even though my medical treatment team tried to make me see through the pains of having PTSD, I didn't have a firm grasp on the illness because I was in so much of a daze. Not even in my prayers could I grasp an answer. I had searched the walls of the psychiatric ward for more than a month, looking for an answer. My walks and my prayers took me long and far, even though I spent most of my time with an escort because I was not fully aware of my own condition. But I had enough insight to know that my worst fears followed me every day.

I knew eventually that I would find the answer to the misery of my life if I could avoid the losses that plagued me daily. Luckily, that day came. I began to read again and stumbled upon a magazine called *Psychiatry Today*. It contained the knowledge of my misery. I was out with an escort one evening and needed a moment to catch my breath. I wanted to read the magazine gingerly, while the escort was dubious about my efforts. I realized, reading this magazine, that I had so many unexpressed emotions that I didn't even know which way to turn. Frantically, I reached for the hidden insights my soul possessed. I desperately wanted to make myself a complete person again.

The memories just would not fade, no matter how much I told myself that I hadn't lived through such a tragic moment. I continued to page through the magazine with my eyes ablaze, looking for the reality I needed to understand. I didn’t recall all the side effects I had experienced over the past two years, but this is what leaped out at me from the magazine as I began to stumble in my reading to find that untold truth.

PTSD triggered unwanted or intense moments of the trauma and nightmares of yesteryear. I remember the burn site in Iraq and heard the screams of several soldiers from the members of my section; it was beyond me to help them. The flashbacks kept occurring. I just could not seem to live in reality. My negative feelings ran wild for no reason at all. Why I put myself through this, I didn’t know. I didn’t deserve this, and nobody else did, either. The memories of combat, death, and killing would not fade. I internally begged for peace of mind, to eliminate the anger within myself, and regain my ability to concentrate. Somehow, I hoped to recapture a former professional lifestyle in the civilian sector.

I sat in total silence. It was too much. Life as I knew it was about to change, but I didn’t know in what direction. Coldness burned within my heart. Not only had I let down the troops in my section in Iraq, but I had let myself down as a leader as well. I didn't know if I had the vigor or strength to deal with this issue on my own, but what made matters worse was that I didn't have that special someone in my life to give me balance and help me overcome the daily growing pains I faced.

When I first embarked on it, I couldn't imagine how arduous this journey would be. I thought it would be easier to end it all right then, but I could not foresee myself as a coward to cheat myself out of any attempt that I had at complete normalcy. I just wanted one chance, but I didn't know if this was going to be real.

One thing that seemed to defy me almost instantaneously was how I would react to the real world once I chose to leave behind this endless voyage of trauma I was on. It was a cycle that never seemed to fade. The issue was called "triggers," and it was an endless problem. I swallowed that word very carefully, not realizing its true potency and how much it would affect me in my upcoming years as I attempted to outgrow the issues that had brought me to Walter Reed.

I began to dream, but I was afraid to let myself go. I was scared of being lost within my troubles for a second time. I was worried to relive the memories of yesterday, the "triggers," as they were called, the mental energies that would set me off without delay. I didn't know if I could get through the mental traumas again. I begged God to spare me the emotions of having to visualize this one more time. Somehow, I snapped out of the oblivious state that I was in. It was thundering outside. This was one of the many things that my psychiatrist advised me to avoid. Even in my older years, I still could not bring myself to listen. Something so meaningless to others was hazardous to me. I couldn't let this punish me, but my inward feeling was that I had no chance. No matter how hard I tried, I could not hide away from the deep and dark feelings that had haunted me in Iraq for many years to come.

I asked the orderly for a piece of fruit or anything to occupy my attention from the nightmare that had just flashed before my eyes. My mind was so weak at this point that I thought this little distraction would help me return to enjoying reality with the rest of the world. I took one bite of the fruit, and within seconds, I spit it out. The fruit tasted like sand, and I thought the orderly was playing tricks on me. My nostrils flared, looking for a fight, but I was too weak to expect even that of myself. At that moment, another orderly entered my room because he had heard the turmoil. I was confused. I didn't want to face the truth; an endless cycle of traumatic insights.

My life had been in the military throughout college and for the first three years of active duty outside the schoolhouse. I thought I would have to be paranoid to follow his orders and live without the basics. The Captain was hitting hard and heavy at this point, but the things he was preaching to me were true. The Captain probably laid out the most important rule of thumb for me. Do not self-medicate and do not abuse alcohol or drugs. This seemed like an easy enough task, but I knew it would stretch my efforts to the max. I had to really think positively to ensure a relentless truth for my own future. I knew it would take a lot of my personal energy to be like everyone else once again, but I would deny myself, no matter how many negatives there were in my life.

This whole thing about having PTSD was starting to get really intense. I was a soldier, and to talk about my feelings associated with the trauma of what happened in combat was against my better judgment. The Captain assured me that breaking through the barriers that isolated me would make me a completely better person. He recommended that I start seeing a talk therapist and check into the possibility of taking medication to help me deal with anxiety and depression. The odd thing about it was that I thought that being a leader of men, I could rise to every challenge, yet this time the challenge was out of my hands. The Captain advised me that the therapy might be done individually or in groups. I just wanted to progress, and I didn't care which way we did it. I didn't know what was best for me, because I spent most of my time working in small groups in the PSC that I was assigned to.

I stared up at the wall. The lecture I had just gotten from the psychiatric nurse/Captain had left my mind on fire, wondering if I would ever erupt again. I wanted to leap back into my uniform, be spontaneous, and find out where my section was. If they had not died, then they deserved the same treatment I was receiving. Despite my ambition, I was still restrained with leather straps for fear of hurting myself.

I could not recall the name of the psychiatrist I would be meeting with, but I knew I could not afford to torture myself throughout the twilight hours at the rate I was going. I looked out the window, hoping to catch a glimpse of the heavens throughout the evening, seeking an answer my heart desired to save me from the desperation that plagued my soul. I never considered myself to be a God-fearing man until I was presented with dealing with the horrors and negativity that I had to now. My life needed to be straightened out like it used to be. Slowly, I drifted into a gentler slumber, refusing to let fear get a hold of me, as it had the previous night.

The following morning, I awoke to a knock from the good Captain. I didn't want to stir, for fear of possibly encountering an unexpected situation. I still had a deep fear burning inside me of an adverse reaction from the previous day's response. I was afraid to confront the unknown. I didn't know what the Captain had on his mind. I was hoping it would be the situation I expected. Dr. Hall then knocked on my door, introduced himself as my healthcare provider, and asked me to come in. I was actually intimidated by the lack of assurance that I could improve my health.

All I could really do was reassure myself that I would do as I was directed and follow through with the guidelines of my medical treatment team. I still thought that PTSD was something that happened in the movies, just not to me. It was tough admitting that I had PTSD, but I guess the issues surrounding PTSD would later have me accepting a serious dose of reality. I was still in a foreign world, trying to convince myself that I would be okay, but down deep, I knew I was just fooling myself.

To me, Dr. Hall was kind of a foreigner. I didn't feel safe. My apprehension was the first thing my doctor noticed. I just wanted to be comfortable with myself at this point, but I was also mentally exhausted and thus unable to voice my concerns to Dr. Hall. He took his time until I became adjusted to him. He was silent, just allowing me to accept his presence. Finally, Dr. Hall took the initiative by asking me how I was doing. I was already on medication for anxiety, so I was slow in my reaction to him, but finally, I overcame my adverse reactions to his foreign presence, and with a strained tone in my voice, I asked Dr. Hall how he was doing. Why I tried to show him proper demeanor, I will never know. Perhaps it was the need to be a professional once again. I didn't know what to expect, but I was reassured there was no hostility and I would still have a future, whether through one-on-one counseling or group counseling. I had decided I was going to have a future, regardless of PTSD.

Dr. Hall was cautious and deliberate in pointing out that my therapy was going to be centered around cognitive-based therapy (CBT) and I would be working very closely with a therapist to help me better understand what I was thinking or feeling about what had transpired in the past. I wanted to deny everything at that point, but I knew I had to be truthful with myself and make honesty a part of my future. Then Dr. Hall went on to advise me about prolonged exposure therapy (PE), which would help me deal in new ways with the thoughts and situations related to the trauma. Breathing and relaxing techniques would teach me how to calm myself when I encounter "triggers." The personal therapist would provide me with a means of improvement when I needed to redefine myself.

This would also improve my coping skills. It would also test my abilities to accept my position in life, and it would provide me with much-needed PTSD psycho-education.

Being in a combat environment had really stressed me out. I had braved so many significant and life-changing events. I didn't know it then, but I have since come to realize how the rest of my life would be affected, especially those close to me. I just never realized how important getting help was going to be for me to manage the upside of my recovery effectively. Letting my family become a central part of my recovery was pivotal. I tried to find former friends in the military, but that was a goal that had no energy and met with no success. Reaching out to www.ptsd.va.gov has eluded me in my goals. I tried to find cohorts in arms who would understand me as a youth and who might be somewhat inclined to understand contemporary issues.

I just wanted to know the truth, but I couldn't explain why I was always on the edge. The nightmares that I dreaded and couldn't avoid were endless, constantly evolving one night after the next. Even with Dr. Hall's assistance, it was a hopeless struggle. The terror had to stop. My resolution to this whole complexity was to spend more and more time at home, away from reality. I was determined to find a resolution for this, to find some peace of mind so that my wife and I could have peace and tranquility together now and forever. Once again, I started therapy at the local Veterans Administration to try to overcome my difficulties. I heard about how good revised treatments were at the VA, but after so many years of a losing battle, I wondered if I had the energy to try again.

To my surprise, I was matched with a therapist who was a master of cognitive-behavioral therapy. My attention was finally piqued. Research shows that CBT is the most commonly utilized therapy for veterans with PTSD. In cognitive therapy, your therapist helps you understand and change how you think about your trauma and its aftermath. Your goal is to know how specific thoughts affect your trauma, cause stress, and make your symptoms worse. My goal, even though I did not think I had any goals then, was to learn to identify thoughts about the world and myself that made me feel afraid or upset with myself.

The therapist made me feel that my treatment was finally being handled in a teamwork environment and my thoughts were more accurate about the PTSD and less distressing. I also learned to cope with anger, guilt, and fear. I quit blaming myself for traumatic events that were beyond my power to change. Cognitive therapy helps you understand that the traumatic event you lived through was not your fault. Perhaps it was time I forgave myself for what had happened in the past. I had tortured my inner self for all those years, and I never really understood why.

For years, I had wanted to say that the mishap in Iraq was my fault for not being more alert, but my therapist made me realize that most accidents in combat happen beyond the control of any level of leadership. Openly admitting that I was being too hard on myself was something I might be able to come to grips with over time. I was battling a personal evil, and only time would tell if I would truly be the complete victor in this battle for my individual soul.

Therapy also helps you control stress and think positively once again. With the guidance of your therapist, you can learn to change how you feel about stressful events over time. Therapy can help you learn to focus on positive memories before taking on the challenges posed by negative thoughts that may be preventing you from progressing. This is called "desensitization," and it helps you deal with the worst memories a little at a time. Your therapist may ask you to remember a lot of bad memories at one time. This is called "flooding," and it helps desensitize you to what it feels like to be overwhelmed. There are many other types of emotional therapy for managing stress and illnesses, such as PTSD, and if you have a therapist in your life, now would be an ideal time to address these issues with them.

Author's Note

Trauma can affect how individuals interpret their spiritual, moral, or ethical understanding of the importance of being accepted as a member of the human race and of the significance of having a personal relationship with God. In the foreseeable future, PTSD will continue to exist as a challenge as our story of the trauma unfolds from the carnage of Afghanistan, Iraq, Operation Desert Shield, Desert Storm, Vietnam, Korea, and even the residual effects of World War II.

Rocket Man

In my life before Vietnam, I felt like I was being led adrift with only minimal guidance. I was like everyone else, waiting for this country's leadership to fulfill us. My parents, in early 1964, were mid-level and worked continuously to try to provide for their family. Little did I know about economics, other than that my father worked extremely hard. I never wanted for anything, and I guess being an only child is what brought that desire on. I easily made friends in high school, or so I told myself, because I was never much of a socialite. My parents tried to help me make up for this deficiency because we spent a lot of time traveling, which allowed me to address any weaknesses.

The Army didn't know it, but they were going to get an actual work of art in 1965. I was determined not to blow the whistle on myself after they drafted me to go to Vietnam, so I decided to let them figure it out that I was a loose cannon on deck. I was in complete self-denial at this point. Despite the patriotic fervor running rampant across the country, I had no zeal for government service or the military after listening to my parents belittle it endlessly, along with their friends. Ironically, the story continues. My dream quest was about to be fulfilled.

Since I really had no flair or desire to serve our government, I always wondered why I didn’t refuse to sign the draft notice. Going to Canada was an option. My father was the reason I didn’t go to Canada. Growing into manhood was an arduous process in 1966, and I knew if I chose to go to Canada, my father would disown me without reservation. He had served patriotically in World War II, and he would expect the same of me in Vietnam without question. Right before I got drafted, life got really interesting for me. I thought I had been blessed with superior intelligence. Boy, did I surprise myself.

Unbelievably, I had just failed out of the local community college. I tried to deny that I could be subject to such an academic blow and was amazed by my own inept capabilities. For some reason, I had put myself out on an academic limb and thought I would like to be an architect. But even though I thought I was so keen, I could not grasp the basic intellectual fundamentals of mechanical drawing. I didn’t understand why I hadn't pursued my passion for automobiles, a passion my parents supported.

My father had such a complete faith in my aptitudes that he thought my abilities were almost obsessive-compulsive. I could look beyond myself when it came to automobiles. I knew all the great race drivers and the type of cars they drove. Perhaps it was obsessive-compulsive, but I just didn’t recognize the behavior pattern yet. My mother was utterly amazed by how I could recall all this insane information about cars and drivers. Yet, she couldn't understand why I would waste my intellectual insights on such trivial details. In hindsight, I should have capitalized on my potential and taken a job at the local gas station after graduating from high school. Even though both my parents admired my knowledge of cars, they were not in favor of my working at the gas station, so off to college I went, and eventually to the draft board.

It was not meant to be my day. The community college made it clear that my services as a student were no longer needed, as I had failed my mechanical design classes. I just hung my head as I walked into the front door of the house, knowing what to expect already. My mother must have been grieving for a period of time while my father had consoled her. That is all that had to be said. Innately, I knew it was my fault. If I had tried harder in school, the pain that was going to be a part of me for the rest of my life could have been avoided. I could only damn my soul and myself for not having been more resilient.

The morning after the finale of my college career, the first phone call I received was from my recruiter. The recruiter was the same for all the new detainees affected by the draft board. The orders were simple and direct: show up at the recruiting station at zero dark hundred to get sworn in. My military occupational skill was given to me at the end of basic training. My new life was centered on being an 11B (an infantryman). My first duty station was at Ft. Knox, Kentucky, for basic training. I had only a working knowledge of Ft Knox, knowing that it held the gold reserve (an actual stroke of genius on that one) and that it was the home to the 3rd Armored Division.

My challenges in Basic Training made me realize that I was a commoner. As the commercial bus rolled into the reception station, my emotions were running rampant. I knew the period from 1965 to 1966 would be the worst eighteen months I would experience. However, I had this distinct feeling that I never realized just how bad it would be. Ninety percent of the recruits were draftees, and most of us were slated for Vietnam. I always hoped there was a typographical error on my orders. I had never ventured out on my own before, let alone for basic training or to prepare myself for the horrors of the war. The scary part was that I had never used a weapon before, and I had never been in any type of hand-to-hand battle, much less what was going to be thrown my way in Vietnam. I was afraid of the inevitable because, for some unknown reason, I followed the politicians' path and believed in the domino theory.

The domino theory was a political strategy to lend credibility to the fight against Communism in Southeast Asia. This was the theory needed to provide momentum to overcome the continual threat of the Viet Cong and the North Vietnamese. At first, I thought that was why I needed to be in Vietnam. However, my views changed as the war progressed, and I came to believe my youth had been wasted. I was so incredibly naïve at that point. However, if I had the energy and willpower to survive basic training, what could Vietnam do to me? Perhaps delusion was a key factor.

Exhilaration ran through my veins the moment the bus doors opened. I had my first experience with a drill sergeant, who had a nasty attitude. The only thing he wanted to do to make his own life easy was to impart some severe pain on as many privates as possible. From Day One through Day Eighty-One, basic training was very intense, from daily calisthenics to the rifle range.

The rigor made me into a machine. Weapons training included the M-14 personal rifle and the M-60 machine gun. Bayonet training couldn't be overlooked, just in case you ever had the experience of going one-on-one in combat with a "gook." I thought the bayonet was the most unique weapon. I really am not a big guy with a lot of power, so outside of practice, I couldn't envision myself using it for anything real. As I quickly found out, the bayonet had limited use for me in combat. I never seemed to run out of ammunition. The most intensive part of basic training was the night infiltration course. I was shocked; with the M-60 gun constantly going off with incendiary rounds, individual troops had to low-crawl 400 meters through concertina wire with flashes going off in bunkers.

Despite being my initial introduction to trauma, basic training turned out to be a very character-building experience. There were many events and activities that I really disliked, but they helped me build my personal and professional character. Physical training pushed me to the limit and really exhausted me on the same days. The more time I spent on marksmanship, the more it improved my abilities. With the M-14, we had to learn to shoot from the standing, cross-sitting, and prone positions. One complicated part for any marksman was stripping the weapon down and cleaning it, but by far the most challenging task was learning the rifle's serial number. Fortunately, I had a memory like a sieve.

As far as learning to respect weapons, the night fire course really taught me the importance of keeping my head down. Finally, the day came, even though I don't talk much about it anymore. It was graduation day, and all the basic training companies were lined up in a massive parade field. One by one, the graduating classes marched by a row of bleachers and executed an "Eyes Right." Every soldier would snap their heads to the right until we had passed the reviewing stand. I was excited like everyone else.

My adrenaline was very much in control now. I was concerned about what my future held. My next duty station was for Advanced Individual Training at Ft. McClellan, Alabama. The first thing I did after I got to Ft McClellan was sign up for an extra week of map training, small-arms assembly and disassembly, and .50-caliber training. I told myself that I should have worked in administration because I finished last in the course, and I was a true putz when it came to weapons.

It didn't take long for the story of assignments to circulate. I didn't have my orders yet, but I knew I was destined to go to Vietnam. There was nothing I could do to prevent the inevitable. I had volunteered for the extra training, so it was a given fact. My ordinary world was about to come to an end. Life went awry when the plane took off for Saigon. There was no cheering, just dead silence. For once, I didn't want to be a hero. When the plane hit the ground in Vietnam, my thoughts were numb: I had no self-expression or feelings at all.

Once the gaggle of troops was off the plane, we passed the time taking in our surroundings, trying to assess where the hell in Vietnam we were. Eventually, we were greeted by a non-commissioned officer. He led us to one of the airplane hangars to get us out of the heat and to give us our orientation of the military base where we were to be stationed. Then came the moment of truth: unit placement. This was not to be my lucky day. I was assigned to Echo Company, 2nd platoon, 3rd squad. My squad leader was Sgt. Mounton from Louisiana, but he wouldn't let you know it. I was in the infantry, and I was about to find out what the infantry was all about.

The company's base camp was at Chu Lai. Simply said, it was a big mother. It had airfields that supported brigade operations. It also had a naval port. We were also thirty-five miles from Tam Ky and about 90 miles from Da Nang. All operations were brigade-, battalion-, or company-size. I was relatively confined to company-sized operations, with most of our companies so depleted by the war that they actually were only platoon-sized elements. I had to give my platoon sergeant a lot of credit, because he was always prepared for any immediate disaster.

My first patrol was with a squad-sized element. We had to cross a swift-flowing stream. In a flash, my squad leader was swept off his feet by the current. Our platoon sergeant threw the end of his rope to Sgt. Mounton rescued him from drowning. I no longer had any doubts as to his sincerity for the platoon and why he carried the rope. The rope had all kinds of uses when we were not deployed in the field. It was a rugged way to start my patrol life in Vietnam.

There seemed to be nothing special about Vietnam or any of our missions. Our missions meant nothing to anyone, including us. We were just a bunch of young men struggling to survive the atrocities of a war that meant nothing to any of us. Recalling the guys' names in our squad was sometimes difficult, though not hard. It left me with an empty feeling when I couldn't recognize the guys who could potentially end up dying with me: the squad leader, Sgt. Mounton, I already knew. Pfc Green, Shepard, and Brown were all riflemen, and the machine gunner was named Grissom. That was only half the squad. My memory can't recall anymore.

Having a personality in Vietnam really didn't pay any dividends. I didn't see why any of the guys made an effort to share their better sides. Only Mounton, Shepard, and Green had any sense of humor, but I still kept my distance. I just had no reason to want to befriend anyone who wasn't going to be part of my life for an extended period. The order was not to make friends. Yet I found no comfort in relying on myself all the time. There was one kid I occasionally found solitude with. His name was Angel Louis Reyes from New York. He prided himself on the M79 he carried. I found confidence in his company, only to find out that he had been brutally murdered in 1968 when he had been sent back to the States. After that, I tried to avoid any serious future friendships.

The infantry in Vietnam favored a wide range of weapons. My favorite was the M-79 grenade launcher. It could shoot a round up to three hundred yards. I mainly used buckshot, high explosive, and tear gas. Charlie hated the M-79s because they were great long-distance weapons, but mediocre for close-up encounters.

PTSD runs rampant in me on some nights. I still have dreams of my first firefight. I distinctly recall the first time our squad contacted the Viet Cong. It was nothing more than a skirmish with a few Charlie. The gunfire was only minor at best. The only casualty that day was the brand-new wristwatch, which I had purchased in Guam. I chuckled under my breath when I realized there were no other casualties at that point.

We had to be constantly wary of snipers. One time, I recall, I was on patrol, and I looked up and saw a sniper in a tree. We saw each other at the same time, but neither of us fired. I would have hated myself if I had killed a kid.

Our first major offensive came against the North Vietnamese. Echo Company had been sent to Tam Ky in January. There were two bridges spanning a river, with a village or town at each end. Our mission was to protect the bridges. The unit had bunkers at both ends of the main bridge that could support heavy equipment and armor. There was a smaller bunker at the end of the smaller bridges where our unit was set to deploy.

There was a rather large tent to the rear of the footbridge. There was about enough space for about twenty guys to rest at one time when they were not on patrol. On January 31, most of the platoon was lying asleep when green tracers came flying through the tent about two and a half feet over our own heads. I flew out of the tent into the bunker. I grabbed the radio and asked for gunship support, only to be told by the dispatcher that none was available at that time.

According to the dispatcher, they were all busy elsewhere. That really left me frazzled. We never went anywhere without gunship support. I didn't know why I was thinking so hard, but with the incidental gunfire and no gunship support, I had no idea what was going on. It didn't matter, as the attack was almost over as soon as it started, but in the midst of things, the tank bridge had been taken out. I did not pride myself on being someone who pays close attention to detail, and this was no exception. I was bewildered by the whole state of affairs. A wise commander kept me from doing an inevitably foolish thing that I would have regretted many years in the future.

The firefights were never-ending from mid-January to the end of June. There was one incident I most directly recall: the platoon came out of a tactical area on patrol across a flat plain. There were no trees or rocks; it was just barren, nowhere to hide if it came to any bombardment. Charlie had waited for the platoon to become exposed entirely, and they opened up on us with mortars. Our platoon was left wide open. Everyone hit the dirt and started firing back. I was holding the radio, so I immediately called for support from the gunships. Within 2 or 3 minutes, I heard the drone of them coming in behind the platoon.

The hovering pilot wanted to know where Charlie was. So, I told him to follow my tracers. Before we left base, I had filled up two mags with nothing but tracers. I loaded up one of my special mags and fired at the jungle that was at the forefront of the platoon. The lead pilot of the three gunships took the right angle and opened up on Charlie. The gunships made two or three passes over Charlie, and then silence fell over the jungle. As usual, I somehow lost myself and didn't really keep calm.

The firefights continued into early summer. It was a dark and dreary night when my squad started up a hill with minimal coverage to our unknown destiny. The rest of the platoon was strung out behind us on the mountain. About halfway up, we began taking fire. My squad leader shuffled to the right, and I went left and started trading fire with Charlie. I engaged the enemy with no solid cover. Every time I saw green tracers, I fired three or four rounds. Eventually, the platoon leader said our efforts were futile and ordered the squad back down the hill. I felt emotional then, because I believed these were the VC that had ambushed the team earlier in the day and killed one of the machine gunners named Gary. I never considered myself to be a vengeful person, but for the first time, I really wanted blood.

The life of the infantryman was never-ending and took an incredible mental toll. I distinctly recall an operation during a seek-and-destroy mission. Group intelligence had informed us where an NVA RPG platoon was holed up. Echo company was working with about 6 or 7 armored personnel carriers (APCs). We approached a sparsely wooded area where the RPG platoon might be in hiding. The tracks (APG's) stopped about seventy yards from the wooded area.

The company was ordered to get on track. When we got within thirty yards, the company dismounted and walked closely beside the track the rest of the way until we drew fire from the NVA RPG platoon. I had the radio and an M-79 grenade launcher. The action between the tracks and the NVA was sparse at best. Yet within a second, one of the tracks was hit by an RPG grenade. The track commander was left for dead on the spot. The battle ended as the others brought their coaxes to bear, squeezed off a few rounds, and the NVA fled the scene. The damage was done. The only thing I wanted was to return to the bivouac and make the most out of a successful day of battle.

The months dragged on with the fear of death constantly by my side. One evening in the QueSohn Valley, my squad was waiting to go out on patrol when I heard the sound of mortars being fired in our direction. Without hesitation, everyone scrambled for a foxhole, except that as a squad, we encountered a significant problem. Since going on patrol/ambush, no one had bothered to dig any foxholes.

One in the distance sent everyone scrambling. The only thing I was able to accomplish was to throw myself on top of someone in it. To make matters worse, somehow four other soldiers had managed to find their way into the hole. My soul was damned when I heard the thuds of mortar rounds hitting closer to the foxhole. I honestly thought I was going to die. Then I saw a soldier crawling towards me, waving for me to let him into the foxhole. I don't know what happened to him, but when the mortars ended, he was no longer visible, and the screaming had stopped.

Meanwhile, a mortar round had landed close enough to set off a CS canister in someone's rucksack. CS is a potent tear gas that makes breathing very difficult. As I choked on tear gas, I thought this was my moment to die. Then there was nothing but silence. Someone with a radio had called for gunship support. Oddly, the mortar attack had skipped over our foxhole. I had been saved by fate. I felt like a ghost on Halloween. I didn't know if that feeling would ever pass.

The patrolling never stopped. It became an obsession with brigade ops to stay on top of Charlie. We had spent two endless weeks pulling patrols from Landing Zone East, West, and Center. The Vietnamese called it the Valley of the Living Dead. I felt the negative energy deep within my bones. Intimidation became a part of me with every step, and hesitation became my middle name. On one of the patrols, I was on point, and my friend Fred Lee had his squad to the right of me, trying to cut through the elephant grass. Elephant grass grows to be about seven feet and will cut your hands or any other exposed body part to ribbons. I had reached my breaking point from swinging a dull machete and finally called for new relief after I experienced muscle failure. Three soldiers were sent to relieve me. The squad moved forward again when it came to a clearing in the grass, stopped for a temporary respite, and then started moving across the open glade. Suddenly, there was an explosion without warning, and I was ready to fight. Fred tried to calm me and nearly got shot in the process. Another buddy pointed out that I had shrapnel in my leg. My personal war was now over, and I had won my Purple Heart.

When I was discharged, there was no end to the reckless abandonment that I wanted to engage in. All I wanted to do was have a good time and smoke weed. I lived in California for three and a half years, living every high for every moment. I got a nice job working in the mailroom of an insurance company, made some friends, and spent every evening riding the highway on my motorcycle. Sometimes at work, I had no recollection of what I was doing. That was my first glimpse of PTSD. By some means, I got along well with most employees, and some of them were even my friends. I still spent too much time alone. That is a way too common issue among combat vets. I really couldn't help myself. There was a crack, sexual trauma from my first wife, and the trauma from Vietnam. My emotions and my life were spinning out of control.

I was really unsure of myself. Combat-related PTSD is more than a trauma; it is a bitch. Most therapists will agree with me on that point. Thanks to modern therapy, I now have a much better understanding of the trauma I saw in Vietnam. I didn't experience any emotional growth while I was there. This partially explains why I would go along with just about anybody to do anything, which led to low self-confidence and low self-esteem, as well as work-related problems.

An Unknown Truth

I didn’t understand why I would cry over little things, and I could function without getting so overwhelmed. Keeping relationships has definitely been the hardest thing. And that goes for any kind: friendships, romantic relationships, my family. That's been a difficult learning lesson. I’ve gotten a lot better because I can tell when I'm not feeling OK anymore. Then I'll just kind of step back, take a breather, and it will work out.

Anything can interrupt my daily routine and make me freak out, even if it’s something minor. Like I had to put air in my tire, and it took five minutes out of my commute to work. Then the panic started, “Oh my God, what is the rest of my day going to be like?” I try to be positive all the time, just to kind of even the odds out. But sometimes it just doesn’t work.

I wasn't really comfortable talking about it to explain to people close to me; I listen, something’s happened, and I don't know what to do, or how to react. Things go through my head, and this is how I respond.

It was just difficult. I found a journal from a couple of years back, and I read it. It was sad- I was hurting myself, I was cutting. I attempted suicide three times before I decided to try to get myself help. After the last attempt, I told someone what I did, and they called Crisis. I ended up at the hospital, and then by the end of the night, I was checked in at a mental health facility. I was there for almost two months, inpatient. I was alone for the first couple of weeks until I figured out where I was, and then it mellowed out.

The cutting was pretty bad before that. I did it on my legs so people wouldn't see. It pretty much went from my knees up. It zigzagged across, and you couldn't tell what was new and what was old. It doesn't look horrible anymore. I didn't wear shorts for a while because I didn't want people to see or ask questions. That used to be a very overwhelming, just people knowing.

Sometimes I get overwhelmed, and my first reaction is to get upset and cry, which worries my co-workers and family. My assistant manager, though, battles with some mental illness himself, so he gets it better. So sometimes it's easier for me to talk to him.

Even before the PTSD, I held a lot of emotions. My childhood was tumultuous. My parents got together at a really young age, found out they were pregnant with me, then married and got pregnant with my brother. My mom was unhappy, so they got divorced when I was four. So, for a while, they were co-parenting really well. We would still go trick-or-treating and do family stuff. But then they both started dating again. My mom started seeing a guy she worked with. We hadn't seen him for a long time; they had been dating for 5 years before we met him. And then my dad started dating a woman whom he met at work. Things were great at first until my dad decided to pursue full custody. And then it went from being with my mom half a week to only being with my mom every other weekend. And that was a big problem for me because I was and am close with my mom; like I'm attached to her hip.

So, when my dad was awarded full custody, something started to get kind of rough for me. I was always grounded. If I got anything below a B in school, I was grounded. C's were two weeks, D's were three weeks, and an F for four weeks. School was not my friend, so I was always grounded.

My dad refused to believe that there was anything wrong with me and that I was acting out for attention or drama, to get my own way, and to be manipulative. But I couldn't focus in school. My mom tried to get help for my ADHD, but he wasn't willing to work with her. So, the doctors couldn't really do anything because he wasn't willing to take extra steps. He had full custody, so it was his decision. So that started to cause a problem. And then I was spending so much time alone in my room because I was not allowed to watch TV, have dessert, be on the phone, or be outside with other kids. I was grounded. So, I was helping make dinner and doing laundry. Like, stuff a normal 12-year-old doesn't really do. And it got to the point that my dad and I weren't getting along whatsoever. I was always in some kind of trouble. He would hit me from time to time.

I used to see a counselor for PTSD when I was first discharged from inpatient. I was there once a week. She was awesome; I loved her, but she left to go to private practice at a facility that didn't take my insurance. My experience after that wasn't great. Her replacement just sat there and looked at my chart and my mental health diagnosis when I went in for a technical college physical. "What makes you think you're going to be a nurse?" she asked. She sat there, and she said, "I'm not your regular doctor, you're un-medicated, and I'm looking at the list of your diagnosis. I don't know if I can sign this physical form saying you're competent enough to go through with this course".

That was the first time as an adult I was told that I could not do something because I had a mental illness. I was so upset when I left that office. I sat in my car for 10 minutes just staring at the cars going by on the road. I didn't know how to process that; she didn't think I was mentally stable enough to pursue that career. I am not a threat to myself or to anyone else. I have a job. I am competent enough to deal with society. Who are you to tell me that I can't go through with a life decision to be a nurse? That was the first time I ever dealt with anything like that. It was hard, and I didn't like that at all. I cried for a day about it because that wasn't what I expected to hear. I literally just needed her to check my vitals and sign a paper. Yet instead, she took one look at my chart without even having a whole conversation with me and said, "No, you can't do that." That was not OK. That's when I realized that there are so many stigmas on mental health, it's ridiculous. She didn't even know what caused my PTSD.

To escape the stifling boundaries at home, I thought it would be a good idea to join the military. I could learn to toughen up there and be the real sergeant in charge. In hindsight, that was not the best decision. I survived Basic Training and wound up deployed in Afghanistan. Interestingly enough, there was a fellow soldier there who looked just like my brother. So, it was like having someone who'd gone through the same experiences I had. Then, one day, out on patrol, he was literally blown to pieces. That image of gore and body parts and spattered blood destroyed me, mentally. I was discharged shortly thereafter.

To Cheat Myself

I took a moment to reflect on what had transpired in my life and had brought me to where I was. I had witnessed the harming of innocent people, and I realized that this was the beginning of the end for me. The shock was more than what I could bear. One of my platoon leaders bragged about saving countless American lives but overlooked the number of lives of foreigners taken in the process. Was this a dream? I hoped I had not given the command to hurt innocent bystanders. Was this the edge of reality, or were my dreams for real? Perhaps this shock explained my new environment and why I felt so empty.

As my career began to spiral out of control, I realized I couldn't define what PTSD was. I had never been in a combat zone before, and it was a tough adjustment recognizing that I needed professional medical help to help me define why my life was out of control. I had no idea as to why my doctor was giving me subtle hints. Little did I know that he was trying to help me and improve my cognitive abilities. My doctor was a warehouse of wisdom, but I didn't listen to the knowledge that he was trying to impart to me. I just refused to listen to his common sense. I was just content to let my life spiral out of control. I had to learn to give myself credit that, over time, I would know what PTSD was the hard way, which is a growing pain I wish I could have been spared.

“CPT Cornell, welcome back,” a voice boomed out, “You were medevacked from the front because of PTSD.”

So, this wasn’t a dream. My thoughts that I was still with my company were wrong. I tried to venture a reply, but my thoughts were scrambled, and my throat was parched. The nurse beckoned me to relax. I was going to experience the growing pains of PTSD as I became more aware, and I could comprehend basic facts again. I didn’t even know where I was at this point, much less able to understand what PTSD was, or why I was strapped to my bed.

My nurse was a warehouse of information, which I just absorbed. Just being in his presence helped relieve the pain. I quickly learned that some of the most common symptoms of PTSD included negative memories or nightmares, sleepless nights, loss of interest in daily activities, or feeling angry. I also could not explain why I was feeling brash. I didn’t really recall whether I had been in a combat zone, but if I had, it didn’t really help my cause, as my outlook on the future continued to grow dim.

I didn’t realize that everything at this point would be such a struggle. PTSD left me in complete agony as I tried to recover the actual cause for myself. I was one of many veterans who would be getting treatment for PTSD and combat stress. I pondered whether this treatment would really work. It was clearly explained to me that the primary tools for the rehabilitation process were therapy and medication, which were essential in helping keep the patient focused on understanding their thoughts and helping me discover ways to cope with my feelings. One of the goals of the medication was to help you feel less worried or sad.

I was informed by my nurse that there can be a wide range of symptoms to indicate that an individual is experiencing signs of PTSD. I was afraid I would feel upset about what happened that caused my emotional disaster. My nightmares had been never-ending and incredibly vivid, which had led to flashbacks and undefined triggers of the negative encounters that drove me into issues that I didn't know how to deal with.

I am not always entirely sure of myself, but I am sure that more than one soldier has been left feeling emotionally cut off from others, living on the edge of fear itself. On many occasions, I have felt numb, as if my heart had been lost, creating insecurity and a loss of interest in my personal and professional passions. I felt depressed at this point, struggling with my inner turmoil. I felt like there was no hope, making me feel very irrational, leading to a feeling of panic.

This was a completely new feeling for me. Perhaps this was due to my new environment, but I wasn't sure. When I was evacuated from the theatre, I was confused and in a daze. It left me afraid and unaware, unsure of my whereabouts. Any noise frightened me. I struggled with my memory. I couldn't recall what had happened. I was in a dream, waiting for someone to tell me what had transpired. I tried to get motivated and get out of bed, but leather straps still bound me in. This was not the time to test my muscular development. My vision was hazy, and for some reason, it was as if I couldn't get anyone's attention to tell me what happened. I wanted to reach out and touch someone, to get them close to me and find out exactly where I was and what had happened to me. Finally, what appeared to be an orderly approached me, but only when I was in a completely exhausted state of mind did they openly say anything to me. In reality, I had no clue what was going on. I couldn't even begin to comprehend that I was suffering from Post-Traumatic Stress Disorder. I was very distressed at that point. I had lived through events that most people couldn't fathom, but I had to face the reality that most other people couldn't either. The pain was out of control at this point, and it was an unreasonable force that penetrated my mind. The agony was building, making me struggle to find reality.

It angered my soul that I had to deal with this personal mental agony by myself. This was a hidden evil that I couldn't share with anyone. The world didn't understand. I was the one suffering, and I didn't even understand the secret horrors of PTSD. It left me feeling so bewildered that there was no more concrete answer to the ailment that left me astray. This was a hidden anger that I couldn't share with anyone. The world didn't understand, and hell, I was the one being punished, and I didn't even understand the hidden horrors that were plaguing me.

Why I was diagnosed with PTSD, I will never know every day brought a new form of mental anguish into my life. I always felt like I was struggling to find an answer to the PTSD. The support team recommended that I confront my fears by writing about them. I wasn't sure this was healthy for me, but I decided to give it a try. I always felt I was damning myself by confronting my fears in such a manner. I didn't know of any other way to address my concerns, and at that point, I wasn't willing to put myself out on a ledge and try anything else, no matter the reason. Not that I was afraid, I was confused and didn't know what was right for me because I was unsure if anyone understood the trauma that was plaguing me. I didn't care who I had to ask for assistance to help me with these issues and the horrors of the past events.

Why I let this issue plague me, I will never know. However, I did realize that this had become more of a truth than one I could deal with on my own. The issue was starting to haunt me in the confines of a world I didn't want to be a part of. Not a night went by that I wasn't feeling on edge. Nightmares kept on pressuring me to no end. I was haunted every night by the atrocities and the negativities of war. My memory was stricken with the violence, and it kept on making me jump when my inner self should have been at peace.

I had only begun to grasp the fears that had embraced my mind. I had experienced something that most people would never understand. I had been placed in danger, and I still had an adverse reaction to the horrors of that night. Perhaps this was a feeling that meant nothing if I was that fortunate. I wanted to read or do something to keep the stressors of the past from haunting my sleep. However, I was afraid to let my guard down, even for a moment. A deep, restless energy kept me from closing my eyes. The clock approached midnight, and my mind was still troubled. I desperately wanted to have peace of mind like everyone else.

Finally, I thought I was about to drift into a gentle sleep, but then fear crossed my mind. I thought I would taste blood again. Explosions ripped through my thoughts as another trip wire scattered them. I knew I had lived through these horrors once, but I was plagued with confusion as to why this was happening again.

I wanted to get up out of the sand, but my paralysis wouldn't let me. I couldn't respond to the cries of my soldiers. My leadership was for not.

I felt a gentle grasp on my shoulder, trying to shake the fear out of me. I was being confronted, urging me to let go of this unwanted fear.

"Sir, it was a trigger in your sleep," she said. I knew what the term helpless was at that point. I searched within my soul and realized I had to outgrow this negativity, this hidden agony, somehow, someway.

I knew I was "safe" in the psychiatric ward at Walter Reed Hospital. I was still petrified by reality. What had happened in the Middle East seemed like yesterday, and my moments of trauma seemed like they had just occurred minutes ago. My brain sensed danger, but my body reacted before I had time to think. I became angry and afraid, just responding to adrenaline and anxiety at this point. I didn't know what made me act so negatively, but it happened very quickly, and it always went to extremes. I didn't even know what triggered the negative memories. What I thought would be an incredible night of sleep had turned into complete horror. I begged myself for an evening of peace and tranquility, but for some unknown reason, I could not accomplish this. I was scared beyond my wit. I didn't want to let any outbursts slip out that would frighten anyone. I was more confused than anything.

The big question for me at this point was "What was the treatment plan for the PTSD?" At this point, things were not going favorably for me, and I needed someone to bring a great deal of brightness into my day. It was as if the nurse had been reading my mind as she brought in my morning breakfast. However, I could not fool myself.

I had not slept a wink all night, and I was in a silent rage. My life seemed to be spiraling at that point, and I was looking for anything that would make my day better. The nurse talked to me in an incredibly polite fashion. I would be having my first workshop on PTSD later that morning. I had been petrified throughout the evening, and now I realized there was a light at the end of the tunnel.

Later on, in the morning, one of the psychiatric nurses calmly approaches my bedside to brief me on the upcoming PTSD treatment. He was a Vietnam-era commissioned officer, which impressed many young leaders like me. The Captain clearly saw the pain in my eyes and the dejection on my face. I was despondent in my initial reaction to him. However, the Captain was a professional determined to take charge of my rehabilitation. I thought this was going to be a relatively brief visit, but within a matter of seconds, I could see that the Captain was determined to give me the best treatment possible. It was going to be a fantastic experience as I learned to conquer the fears of the previous night.

The Captain wasted no time in talking about the "triggers" of the previous night. He was forthright in his narration, not wasting any time in addressing the issue. He was direct and to the point, saying that I should avoid people, places, and things that reminded me of the trauma. My triggers were psychological at that point, and the nurse taught me how to be direct with them.

Most people have never realized that life in the war zone is so much different from life at home. My daily routine had been interrupted by something more stressful and chaotic than most people will ever experience. The events surrounding my military life had driven me to the edge and beyond. My only reaction was to hide my feelings about the stress around me. Even though I was safe in the hospital, I was being haunted by nightmares and unwanted memories of what had transpired.

Memories of that explosion dominated every waking moment. I was angry and blamed myself for not seeing the trip wire. My thoughts were dominated by ignorance because I let it replace my better judgment. I hated myself for not being more aware. Even though I was an officer, I could only damn my soul for not being more responsible. At first, the good captain was in complete silence for the longest period. Little did I realize that I was being closely observed to see if I was caught up in my own emotions. I was caught up in my own insanity and did not realize the intent of others who were trying to help me.

The Captain was quick to say in a somewhat oblivious fashion that I was experiencing symptoms of PTSD. Still, he couldn't explain why I was keeping my feelings bottled up within me and why I couldn't release the negativity. Despite the trauma I had to deal with, I hoped I could eventually overcome the haunted side of my life. Even though my medical treatment team was trying to make me see through the pains of having PTSD, I didn't have a firm grasp on the illness now because my temperament was in a daze. Not even in my wildest dreams could I grasp an answer. I could hope to find an answer to my growing pains. I knew at some point that I would find the answers to the misery of my life if somehow I could avoid the losses that plagued me daily. Luckily, that day came. I began to read beyond myself because it helped me avoid an untold misery. Oddly enough, I broadened my horizons by stumbling upon a magazine called Psychiatry Today. It contained the knowledge that would cure me of my misery. I quickly realized, by reading this magazine, that I had so many unexpressed emotions at this point that I didn't know which way to turn. Frantically, I reached for the hidden insights that my soul possessed. I wanted so desperately to be myself as a complete person. I tried to express my feelings to my psychiatric team once again and to somehow make myself whole once again, but there seemed to be no apparent connection. Damn my soul for allowing me to become such a disheveled mess.

I began to reminisce at this point. The memories would not fade, no matter how hard I tried to convince myself that the tragedy would disappear. I continued to page through the magazine, my eyes ablaze, looking for the reality I needed to understand. I didn't recall all the side effects I had experienced over the past several years, but I knew that somehow, I needed to make a change.

PTSD triggered the negative emotions within me, only having scarred emotions relating to yesteryear. I remember the burn site in Iraq and the screams of scarred soldiers. It was beyond me to help them, let alone help myself. The flashbacks kept recurring. I just could not seem to live in day-to-day reality. My negative feelings ran wild for no reason at all. I had the most intense memories in which I could not break out of my shell to make myself a complete person again. I was reliving the moments of misery, no matter how intense my feelings were. Why I was putting myself through this, I didn't know. I didn't deserve this, and nobody else did either. The memories of the combat zone, the death, and killing would not fade away. I was intensely begging for peace of mind at this point.

I couldn't eliminate the anger within myself. I struggled to regain my ability to concentrate at this point, even though I was regaining strength to deal with the issues that had plagued me before. Somehow, I hoped I might be able to recapture a former lifestyle as a professional in the civilian sector, because no matter how hard I tried, I never found peace as a military officer, especially with my growing pains.

I just sat there in total silence. It was too much. Life as I knew it was about to change, but I didn't know in what direction. Coldness burned within my heart. I had let myself down as a leader. I didn't know if I had the vigor or strength to deal with this issue by myself, and what made matters worse was that, for some God-forsaken reason, I didn't have that special someone in my life to give me the balance I needed to help me overcome my daily growing pains.

When I first embarked on it, I couldn't imagine how arduous this journey would be. I thought it would be easier to end it all right then and now, but I couldn't force myself to be a coward and cheat myself out of the chance to become an actual person once again. I just didn't want to face the negative reality of having a mental illness.

One thing that seemed to defy me was a positive reaction to the real world. I wanted to leave this endless cycle of trauma behind. The issue was called "triggers," and it was an infinite problem. I swallowed that word every day, not realizing its true potency or how much it would affect me in the years ahead. I didn't know what the twilight was going to bring into my life at that point.

I was mentally exhausted and afraid to let the evening take me away from my supposed troubles. I just stared up at the wall. My thoughts were so scrambled at this point. What did I ever do to deserve this internal hell? I wanted to sleep, but my mind was ablaze, and I was too afraid even to close my eyes. My mind was on fire, wondering if I would erupt again.

I closed my eyes as my body was begging me for sleep. I couldn't escape the inevitable. I remember the trauma that had left me frozen in fear. I couldn't escape the inescapable. I remember the trauma that had left me frozen in fear, no matter what the circumstances. How do I confront the trauma from this point forward? I had to be honest with myself because no one else would. Being in a combat environment had really stressed me out. I had been forced to brave so many significant and life-changing events.

I didn't realize how much this would affect the rest of my life. I just never looked beyond the new boundaries and how important it is in getting help to manage my future and contribute to my recovery effectively. At this point, I was willing to reach out beyond myself and include the necessary time that I would need to recover from and combat my trauma. I didn't know how to navigate this course on my own. Letting my family become a central part of my recovery was pivotal at this point. I reached out to myself to try to find former military friends. That was a goal I had no energy for and failed to achieve. Reaching out to www.ptsd.va.gov was unsuccessful. I tried to find cohorts in arms who would understand me as a youth and who might be somewhat inclined to appreciate my contemporary issues.

Conclusion

I felt on edge night after night as I struggled endlessly to find the medical answer that eluded me. I couldn't avoid the truth and pain of the matter. The nightmares just kept coming back one night after the next. I didn't know if I could survive this onslaught. Sudden noises always set me on edge. I was too afraid to include moments of reality in my life. My mind was always defying me, and I really had to guess if this was really PTSD, or if I was just overreacting and making an excuse for myself. It shook me that I was acting as if I were weak and out of control.

I felt like I was no longer in control. I didn't feel like other people who could make unbridled decisions without hassle or heartburn. I couldn't bring myself to understand at this point why things were the way they happened to be. I wondered if this was just something I had to endure conditionally. I could only damn my own aggressiveness, or my rampant thoughts, and my inability to better myself and become a better part of society once again.

I just wanted to know the truth as to why I was always on edge. The nightmares that I dreaded and couldn't avoid haunted me endlessly, one night after the next. Even with the assistance of the medical treatment team, I could not find peace of mind. It was an endless struggle, where sudden noises left me entirely on edge.

When will the terror stop, and when will I see a peaceful resolution? Somehow, the terror had to stop. I was avoiding reality for no apparent reason. I could only feel within my heart that the trauma would end, but I couldn't avoid it.

I was determined to find a resolution for this, to find some peace of mind so that I could appreciate the tranquility once and forever. Once again, I started therapy at the local Veterans Administration to tackle the unknown to see if I had the energy to move my life forward.

I would not be denied.

References

1. The Walking Wounded – PTSD from Ancient Greece to Afghanistan." http://militaryhistorynow.com/2012/09/17/walking-wounded-ptsd-from-ancient-greece-to-afghanistan/
2. Battle Fatigue, Post-Traumatic Stress Disorder, Combat Stress." http://www.schwab-writings.com/bm/bf/Fatigue.html.
3. Baur, P. (2015). "The Future of Trauma"

www.ingramcontent.com/pod-product-compliance
Lightning Source LLC
LaVergne TN
LVHW022050200926
848481LV00003B/847
* 9 7 9 8 2 9 5 6 3 7 0 6 3 *